The Hidden Addiction

The Hidden Addiction

Behind Shoplifting and Other Self-Defeating Behaviors

... and How to Reclaim Your Life and Self-Respect

PETER BERLIN

NEW YORK

The Hidden Addiction
Behind Shoplifting and Other Self-Defeating Behaviors
... and How to Reclaim Your Life and Self-Respect

ISBN 978-1-61448-390-8 paperback
ISBN 978-1-61448-391-5 eBook
Library of Congress Control Number: 2012949121

Morgan James Publishing
The Entrepreneurial Publisher
5 Penn Plaza, 23rd Floor
New York City, New York 10001
(212) 655-5470 office • (516) 908-4496 fax
www.MorganJamesPublishing.com

Cover Design by:
Chris Treccani
www.3dogdesign.net

Interior Design by:
Bonnie Bushman
bonnie@caboodlegraphics.com

In an effort to support local communities, raise awareness and funds, Morgan James Publishing donates a percentage of all book sales for the life of each book to Habitat for Humanity Peninsula and Greater Williamsburg.

Get involved today, visit
www.MorganJamesBuilds.com.

Habitat
for Humanity®
Peninsula and
Greater Williamsburg
Building Partner

Table of Contents

Inspiration

"I am so ashamed," said one woman who shoplifted. "I'm a good Christian. I was never in trouble before. How could I do such a thing? I can't believe I did this and put myself in this position. How can God ever forgive me? What am I going to do now?"

"Even looking back now, I have no idea why I did it."

"I was having trouble at home," said another woman who shoplifted. It wasn't for the lack of money or anything like that; it was as if it was an addiction ... the rush or high was so intense... the feeling of getting away with it. It is like an addiction to a drug. I didn't feel I could help myself."

"Shoplifting for me was like taking a little control back in my life."

Another woman noted, "I was a teenager at the time and I did it because it was something everyone else was doing. As I got older it was something once I started doing, the thrill of doing it and the rush of getting away with it made me want to continue."

"I am so ashamed of what I did."

People's self-defeating behaviors frequently do not reflect who they truly are as human beings but rather what they were temporarily driven to do as a result of early hurtful experiences, self-inflicted wounds and loss of hope.

This book helps to explain why so many decent people become involved in self-defeating behaviors of all kinds like alcohol, drugs, overeating, shoplifting, compulsive shopping, anorexia and more. It offers a way for people to resolve their internal conflicts so they can turn self-defeating behaviors in their life into self-nourishing behaviors.

This book was inspired by what I observed from the self-defeating behavior of those people caught shoplifting. After spending the first twenty years of my retail career locking-up shoplifters and dishonest employees, as well as consulting with more than 100 retailers worldwide in regard to security and loss prevention, I saw a great need for individual intervention to get people back on track. This is because so many otherwise decent people were stealing store merchandise and had "no idea" why they needlessly put themselves in this position. After a time I didn't only see them as thieves but also as PEOPLE. With that in mind, I founded a non-profit organization named the National Association for Shoplifting Prevention (NASP), originally formed as Shoplifters Anonymous, Inc. This organization, founded in 1989, has assisted over 300,000 people by working with individuals, retailers, courts and agencies to prevent, re-educate and rehabilitate people who shoplifted.

For this reason, I have walked a path no one else has walked in the same way.

With my own formal education in Psychology, my work with clinical psychologists and my 40+ years of practical hands-on experience, I learned how self-defeating behaviors develop and how to help break the cycle and shift people's life choices in a positive manner.

Self-Defeating Behaviors Other Than Shoplifting

The statistics support that millions of otherwise decent people do foolish and harmful things for reasons even unknown to them. They indulge in such things as excessive overeating, gambling, alcohol, drug use, anger and rage, anxiety and depression, compulsive shopping, bulimia, anorexia, sexual misconduct and other self-defeating behaviors. These people are attempting to "self-medicate" in various different and often harmful ways in an attempt to reduce their emotional pain in life and help themselves feel better. In time, their behavior acts as a substitute for coping with life in more realistic and effective ways. Eventually their behavior can develop into a habit or even an addiction. Many people also develop dual addictions when only one self-defeating behavior alone does not satisfy their emotional needs.

These types of behaviors are not the real problem for anyone but are rather only a signal or symptom of an underlying issue. There is always something deeper within the individual that is compelling him or her to negatively act out. These can include insecurity, disappointing love relationships, feelings of being controlled, problems at home, lack of self-esteem or self-worth, anxiety, depression, loss of a loved one, poor health, and the loss of hope. People are either not aware of or do not identify the connection between important underlying life issues and the behaviors that inevitably result. They become committed to their ideas and create what becomes an inner hidden addiction. They feel compelled to act on the ideas they hold, even if those ideas may prove harmful to them and result in self-defeating behaviors.

A HIDDEN ADDICTION exists when you are not aware that you have become so dependent on something or someone that you must always act to satisfy your dependence.

As a result, people often place themselves in a compromising position and ultimately suffer the consequences of their actions. While it is certainly no person's intent to make his or her life more difficult, without a person's awareness of what may unknowingly be going on inside, they have no clear direction, have less chance for change, are less likely to remedy their future actions and therefore are more likely to repeat their behavior.

This book does not deal with a "prescription addiction" which is the result of a physical dependence from a legally prescribed substance because the root cause of this type addiction is not emotional in nature.

This book was inspired by the idea and the hope that helping people to overcome hidden addictions will simplify their struggles and motivate people just like you to gain a greater measure of understanding, comfort, stability and happiness for the remainder of their life. As concerns shoplifting, the problems of retail security, the crime of shoplifting, the cost to retailers and consumers, the hardships on the police, the courts and the jails, as well as the moral aspects of shoplifting, are not the subject of this book. This book uses shoplifting as an example of how otherwise decent people (not professional criminals), who either had a rough start in life or have made their own life harder along the way, can find the way to get back on track and reclaim their life and self-respect.

Acknowledgments

Deep appreciation is expressed to the dedicated people at the National Association for Shoplifting Prevention (NASP) and my wife Meryl, daughter Caroline and son Michael for supporting me in using a good portion of our life savings to start a non-profit organization and help to fulfill an idea and a hope. Also, deserved recognition to Max Harris, Ph.D, the clinical psychologist who offered his assistance in NASP program development and clinical matters, Robert C. Lane, Ph.D for his guidance and support on the Board of Directors and Kathy Bacon, Ph.D for her contribution in developing NASP curriculums and her help with the research and field work.

Grateful acknowledgment is also given to Richard Jorgensen, Ph.D (hc), at www.LifeSkillsU.com, author, mentor and Life Coach who has mentored and assisted me in developing and expanding some of the concepts used within this book.

Introduction

A person caught shoplifting said to me, *"Would you believe I am a Clinical Psychologist with two beautiful young daughters. I am setting a horrible example for them by shoplifting. I have tried to cope with my health and marital problems but I can't escape from my anxiety and depression. The added stress that has come from my new legal issues is terrible. I am not built for this. I haven't eaten or slept since I was arrested two months ago."*

I probably don't need to tell you how people's lives can become complicated and appear to spiral out of control. When experiences occur which threaten your safety or security, love, independence or self-worth, your life can feel overwhelming and complicated. Ultimately, your response can easily be an overreaction to the stress.

The same stress, overreaction and inability to cope that lead people to shoplift are also replicated in other self-defeating behaviors. The good news is that life, like all complex things, also has a universal simplicity.

The recognition of this simplicity can help you to reduce your personal struggles. By opening your mind to the advice and guidance you will read in this book, you have a great opportunity to change in any way you wish.

The reason people can simplify their struggles in life is because life's struggles are not the result of the behavior of others but rather your response to the behavior of others. Therefore, the solution to your struggles is always in your hands.

Throughout this book, you will find many thoughts and ideas to prompt you to reflect on how these thoughts may apply to you. However, a word of caution:

Regardless of the fact that I am an acknowledged expert in my field, the first and perhaps most important thing I want to tell you is:

I do not want you to trust me.

What I want from you is a promise that you will only *trust yourself.*

In life you must learn to trust your instincts. You can trust what I say only if YOU believe that what I say and the way I say it makes sense and feels right for you. Regardless of where you are right now in your struggle with life and regardless of whether you believe you are capable, I want you to trust only your feelings and judgment.

My hope is you will view this book as a way to find the real truth regarding unanswered questions about your past, your current beliefs and the corresponding behaviors that ensue. If you are living an illusion, you need to know the truth. To know what is real for you, you can only rely on yourself.

Through our journey to help you find your real truth, you will then begin to shift your decisions and behaviors to those that enhance your life, rather than hurt it.

In order to find the real truth, you must be able to trust yourself because you are ultimately the best judge of what is right for you. Everyone is unique and what you feel is best for you may be different than someone else's feelings. Even if you have lost some confidence in yourself along the way because of past behaviors, this book will help you to regain your confidence and instill a pattern of positive decisions and beneficial outcomes.

Each chapter in this book is designed to take you through part of a "process" for discovering the real truth about you. Obtaining the ability to see yourself and your world from a realistic perspective will help resolve most of the issues you will ever face. In essence, this book will largely guide you to remain aware and balance your natural inner wisdom with your outer experiences, a skill we all need to perfect.

Ralph Waldo Emerson said: *"All the religions of the world, while they may differ in other respects, uniformly proclaim that nothing lives in this world but Truth."*

Mr. Emerson's quote says to me that there is always a truth and we must find it and accept it, for not knowing or denying the truth does not make it go away.

Through using shoplifting as an example of the many self-defeating behaviors, the forthcoming chapters are carefully designed to effectively help you dig out the root of any problem and transform it or discard it forever. Even though you may be anxious to quickly find a better solution for you, please don't rush the "process" but rather allow yourself to slowly absorb and use what you can and begin to implement new thoughts into your everyday life. You may have heard parts of what you will read here but you now need to fully understand their meaning to your life.

To prevent you from wondering what lays ahead, the "process" begins with an awareness of shameful secrets and false beliefs about yourself that you hold in both a conscious and unconscious manner. These ideas can hold you hostage. Many people carry beliefs about themselves (usually acquired from others) that are simply not true. As a result, their lives are unsettled because they are consistently influenced or guided by shameful secrets and false beliefs. Regardless of the secrets and false beliefs you hold from your past, the next step will be to reflect on who you really are as a human being, in order to accurately recognize and accept the *real truth* about you.

Once you are secure in yourself and self-worth, the entire process will move faster and any changes you wish to make are almost guaranteed.

The "process" will later reveal how to replace any false beliefs you hold about yourself to ensure your life is anchored into reality and not illusions.

The remaining chapters will discuss the challenges we all face in life, the things you need and don't need, who and what can you trust, how to find harmony with your daily experiences, how to direct and replace anger and identify and implement your true "Guidance System."

As you read, keep in mind your ultimate goal. It may be giving up a specific negative habit, releasing your depression, reducing awkward behavior, regaining your self-respect or re-instilling your hope in life.

Since some of the material in this book may require deep inner reflection and thought, I have purposely repeated key thoughts throughout the book. At times, you may find it helpful to pause and consider what you just read.

As you are reading the chapters you may find yourself saying 'What does this have to do with my problems?" The answer is that everything in this book relates to overcoming self-defeating behaviors. While every concept may not apply directly to you today, it might apply to you tomorrow so you need to understand *everything* that is being presented to you.

Finally, write down questions or notes in the margins of this book so that you are interacting with the material rather than just reading it.

When you have completed reading this book, you may email any questions you have to the author at **Peter@PeterBerlinAddictionCoach.com** and you are promised to receive a reply.

CHAPTER 1

Your Big Secret

"Nothing weighs so heavily on us as a secret."
—Jean de La Fontaine (1621-1695) French poet.

Self-defeating behaviors often develop because shameful secrets are given too much importance by the holder of the secret and thereby inhibit these individuals from moving forward.

Don't allow secrets you hold to haunt you throughout your life.

There are millions of people whose innermost secrets continue to torment them on a daily basis. In their eyes, their secret(s) must be buried and never revealed to others for fear of embarrassment, rejection and shame.

Many people live with their secrets for the entirety of their lives. Personal secrets you carry about yourself can frequently limit your personal success and growth. They need to be resolved (by you) before you can move forward with your life.

These secrets might include:

"I have a criminal record or I spent time in prison"

"I cheated to get a job"

"I don't expect to amount to anything because my father told me so"

"I lied and got someone else in deep trouble"

"I watched someone being physically abused and did nothing"

"I stole money from my grandmother"

"I left the scene of a serious accident"

"I am a shoplifter"

"I betrayed my best friend"

"I had an extramarital affair"

and more…

Most of these secrets are often deemed shameful and cause people to feel like a cheat, fake or coward. With those feelings comes a subconscious inner belief they are an unworthy person. This feeling then causes people to sacrifice many things throughout their life they would otherwise pursue and enjoy. For example, people who feel unworthy often feel less deserving of positive things, are willing to accept less in life, are reluctant to acknowledge their accomplishments and even find trouble in accepting compliments from others because their inner-voice says quietly to others, "you don't really know what or who I am."

Does any of this resonate with you?

People with these types of secrets consider their shameful act is a reflection of their true character as a person. In truth, these acts are much more a reflection of what you did under emotional or physical stress, rather than who you really are as a person.

There is a big difference between what you did and who you are. Seeing the difference is vital to your growth. Don't condemn your entire being for one or two acts of indiscretion. We have all made decisions we regret but that does not make us a bad person. Rather, it reflects a poor choice at a given time for any number of possible and often understandable reasons (not excuses).

The emotional stress leading people to shoplift, to overeat, become a shopaholic or gamble is the same thing causing other self-defeating behaviors. The result may be different, but the origin is not.

One of the main purposes of this book is to free you from your big secret which may have led to your self-defeating behaviors, so you can resolve this issue within yourself forever.

While you might think, 'I would never shoplift or take drugs because I would be too scared,' don't underestimate the power stress can have on your life. Enormous stress can cause otherwise good people to make poor judgment calls and change their behaviors from self-fulfilling behavior to self-defeating behavior.

That being said, almost everyone has some secrets or false beliefs they hold about themselves and if they can shed those secrets and false beliefs and replace them with the real truth, their life will immediately change for the better. This book will offer you those real truths.

People often think that it is not going to be easy to change a belief they had for years. However, I can assure you that once you accept the real truth, your belief will change instantly.

As an example, imagine you work in an office and there is a co-worker in your department named Lori whom you never liked since she first began working with you three years ago. Lori is unfriendly, rarely smiles, prefers to keep to herself, never volunteers to help, takes lunch by herself, leaves at the stroke of 5:00 PM every day and rarely offers to pitch-in if others are trying to meet a deadline. She is just not a team player.

One day while having a drink after work with a friend from another department, you learn that Lori has been fighting multiple sclerosis for the past five years, that she volunteers in a children's shelter two nights a week after work and is a single mother with two girls to care for at home.

After three years, your opinion of Lori immediately changed and you now feel less judgmental and more kindly toward Lori. Your earlier belief about Lori turned from resentment to compassion in a matter of seconds.

This is an example of how quickly you can change a long held belief and it is the same with beliefs from childhood when you finally see and accept the real truth.

Madeline Albright, former US Secretary of State put it this way:

"What people have the capacity to choose, they have the ability to change."

Another Kind of Secret

There is another kind of secret about yourself that you may not be aware of but which is directly tied to the happiness and success in your life. It may not appear to be related to shoplifting or other self-defeating behaviors - but it is. We are talking about those hidden beliefs you hold about yourself which are "false" and "untrue" - thereby making the real truth (about you) a secret to you.

Here are common examples of things people subconsciously believe about themselves that lead them down the wrong path:

"I can never make up for hurting my kids because I was an addict"

"I will never be good enough in the eyes of my father (or mother)"

"I will never be as pretty as my sister or as smart as my brother"

"I can never forgive myself for having an affair with my boss"

"I feel so guilty because I did not protect my baby sister"

"After my divorce, I don't feel I can ever marry again"

"I feel everyone is trying to control me"

"I am a disappointment to everyone"

"I am too frightened and insecure"

"I am not deserving of nice things"

"I am not worthy of being loved"

"I can never do anything right"

"I feel guilty about everything"

"I am ashamed of my body"

"I am so unsure of myself"

"I was never really loved"

"I am truly alone"

After further reflection, what are the negative ideas about yourself you believe are true? As you will soon discover, in almost all instances, all these kind of beliefs are either inaccurate, not your fault, or unimportant to both you and your life today. They have had meaning to you in the past and can appear devastating, but they don't need to be.

Both the secrets you are aware of but falsely believe to be true and, the hidden secrets you are not consciously aware of are both important issues because they can independently have a damaging and unhappy influence on your life.

Leroy Robert "Satchel" Paige, the great major league baseball pitcher and first black player to be inducted into the Baseball Hall of Fame, put it this way:

"It's not what you don't know that hurts you; it's what you know that just ain't so."

If you are a person who shoplifts, for example, you are well versed in the many negative things about shoplifting, yet you still do it.

So, the question remains: What is it that you don't know?

The first step to shifting your behavior is understanding the root of the problem. With that said, the best way to understand yourself and your conditioning is by reflecting on the following questions and mark your answer in the margin:

- Do you believe the actions of other people are the reasons for much of your present difficulty in life?
- Do you believe your early life and past experiences determined your future?
- Do you believe since the past actions of others cannot be undone, your past difficulties also cannot be fixed?
- Do you believe the losses or hurt you experienced in the past left a hole within you that cannot be filled?
- Do you believe you are a victim of circumstance?
- Do you believe you give more than you get back?
- Do you believe that for your life to change for the better, others will also have to change?

If you answered "yes" to any of these questions, this book will begin to change your life. If you feel you are completely in control of your life, your answer to every question would have been "no." If your answer was "yes", we need to dive deeper and evaluate further. This book will help you gain greater freedom from what you perceive as harmful and irresolvable influences on your life.

SO, What Is The Wisdom In This Chapter and ... What Do You Do With This Information?

Some of these comments are redundant but I believe are also necessary reinforcement.

Your secrets need not haunt you throughout life. There was a specific reason (not an excuse) why things happened the way they did and you need to open your eyes and mind to see the real truth about you. This will allow you to release guilt or shame and replace it with understanding and a real reason to forgive yourself. I would guarantee the real truth is not going to be as bad as you now imagine.

What is important to understand is without knowing the real truth about yourself; you are making some decisions based on an illusion.

As we move together on this journey try to keep your mind open rather than make snap judgments as you read.

Question what you think you know that maybe "just ain't so".

Allow yourself to replace your current belief with a new belief if you learn something new. This will completely destroy the old false belief.

Try to avoid the temptation to immediately deny what is written here in order to defend yourself because ... you are not being judged.

Try to put your hurt, blame, anger or guilt aside temporarily so you are not committed to holding onto your present beliefs from your past.

Our only goal here is to think about your well-being and not worry about what others think or how others may react to you if you change in some way. The focus here is only on you. Also, please do not rush to find an answer to your specific problem, as finding an answer will come at the end of the process.

CHAPTER 2

Who Are You?

Most importantly, who do you think you are?

What you think and believe about yourself is ultimately the most important factor in determining how almost all experiences will affect your life, both positively and negatively.

Self-defeating behaviors are permitted to take hold in people who falsely believe that they are somehow broken, damaged or defeated and therefore unable to rise to what otherwise would be their true self.

Therefore, it is essential for you to recognize the truth about your personal self-worth. This chapter will help you to become crystal clear regarding who you really are, independent of what people told you or any decisions you made in your past that had negative effects on your future.

You are not a result of your decisions regarding shoplifting, drug use, alcohol abuse, excessive gambling or other self-defeating behaviors. You are a result of what you believed at the time which led you to those decisions.

The Father of American Psychology, William James wrote: *"There is but one cause of human failure. And that is man's lack of faith in his true self."*

You know that people who don't believe they can accomplish something will not even try to accomplish it, thereby making their belief a self-fulfilling prophecy.

It is the false beliefs you hold about yourself and others that allow you to continually make poor decisions. However, within this book are powerful thoughts and principles that will empower you to gain strength in shedding false beliefs. If you have shoplifted or otherwise felt you disgraced or dishonored yourself in some manner, you undoubtedly feel some guilt and shame. You may also believe that you are an unworthy person who deserves less than others because of the mistakes you made. And, you may not know how you can ever forgive yourself for doing what you knew was wrong and against your core beliefs in the first place.

These types of feelings alone speak to the goodness within you.

Simultaneous with these feelings of remorse should come the recognition you are not a career criminal or hurtful person and that you spent much of your life trying to do the right thing and make positive choices. At times, you have been very proud of yourself. However, if you engaged in self-defeating behaviors and were unable to stop yourself, you may also feel a sense of guilt and shame and therefore may incorrectly conclude there must be something really wrong with you. This is almost always not the truth.

Mahatma Gandhi once said, *"There is no God higher than truth."*

I believe he meant for everyone to seek the truth about all things.

While I don't know you personally or are familiar with your beliefs, because we are both human beings, there is far more that unites us than separates us. As an example, we both have physical needs and emotional needs which are unique but also remarkably similar as human beings. Due to my intimate experience with people who shoplift or engage in other self-defeating behaviors, I do know the truth about you.

Without ever meeting you, I can know who you are. That is because as a human being, you are very much like me. I don't want to appear arrogant but you are a human being who was created by "God" and "Mother Nature" (as you prefer) and you and I were given, at birth, all the things we need to evolve, grow and prosper throughout our life or we couldn't sustain ourselves. To be clear, I am not speaking about the religious God but rather the universal God within all religions. If you are an atheist or agnostic, the wisdom in the world simply has a different origin for you. I simply use the word "God" throughout this book as a word to describe the wisdom that exists in our world, rather than a specific religious affiliation or belief.

You may choose to believe anything you wish about yourself but, in reality, there were powerful forces which some call "God" or "Mother Nature" that created you as part of the wisdom in our world. Regardless of how hard you try to believe one thing or another about yourself, please accept that the powerful truth that you do not have the ability to change those precious things about you that had already been created before birth. However, as you move forward in life, you do have the freedom and ability to make choices about how to live a fulfilling life.

Some people may be at a place in their life where they wonder why they were ever born. They may say, "What good has it done? How is the world better? I brought two children into the world and they are going to have it harder than I did. I don't think God is always right. There are too many problems in the world and it doesn't seem to be getting better."

While I understand how some people might feel they have little value to both themselves and others, this is almost never true. As history shows us, while the world outside you will always be in turmoil, the value of your life is the goodness you bring to the world. This is why the world has never been overrun by evil.

Now, let's look at the real you. Are you ready?

Looking at the real "you" may be difficult because you already formed certain beliefs about yourself based largely on either what others told you or how you interpreted the emotional feedback you received from those surrounding you. This is how you consciously and unconsciously formed your beliefs so you could survive in the best way you knew how. No fault in that. However, today you are an adult and possess the ability to decide which of your current beliefs from the past are positive and true and those that are negative and false.

Please remember that your beliefs, particularly those about yourself, were formed after birth based on the actions and words of others. As an adult you have a responsibility to continually question the truth or legitimacy of the concepts you were led to believe. If we all don't question the beliefs formed early in life, we will continue to carry false beliefs about ourselves. This leads to poor life choices and the negative results that go with them. With that said, here is your first big truth to consider:

When you were born, you entered this world as a *perfect human being*. You carried genetic and physical differences from others, but you were born exactly as God and Mother Nature intended you to be. You started off *perfect*. Even though you may have been born with certain physical limitations or issues, (born with four toes or three eyes) your inner beauty and character were flawless. It is a rare thing to find any infant who is not precious, lovable, innocent, and just a miracle of nature—including you.

You may believe that you were never perfect but I'll wager that you cannot tell me one thing about you as a human being that was imperfect when you were born. Not a single thing. So why believe something about yourself that is just not true?

You can never change the fact you were born perfect because it is a constant throughout your life. In fact, there is nothing you can do to alter Mother Nature and God's creation, no matter what you do. So, if you want to believe the real truth about you, you would be wise to accept the fact you were born as a perfect human being. This may be difficult for you to accept based on the negativity you experienced through life, but it is true.

The word "perfect" has strong meaning. Most people don't see themselves as perfect. In this context, "perfect" means you were not flawed as a decent human being in any way when you were created. This is how you started the game of life.

So the question remains: if you started life with a clean slate as a perfect human being, at what point did you change into an imperfect human being? The answer may surprise you: *You never did become imperfect.*

A big stumbling block with people accepting they are naturally perfect is they say to themselves, "As hard as I try, I just can't ever see myself as perfect."

My response is to flip this thought around and explain to me why you see your being as anything but perfect? It is obvious you were born perfect because of the things you genuinely feel reflecting your goodness within:

- You care about others
- You don't want to hurt anyone or see anyone hurt
- You have spent much of your life trying to do good
- You feel guilt about wrongs you have done
- You are ashamed by some of your past behaviors
- You enjoy seeing your loved ones happy
- You are unhappy when others are sad
- You like to give to others
- You get joy from the joy of others

- You feel sorrow, guilt or shame when you do the wrong thing which clearly speaks of the goodness within you.

Many of these feelings didn't come from others, but rather are a reflection of who your really are, which speaks so loudly about you that people often can't hear anything else you might be saying.

If you choose to believe the absolute truth that you are not flawed in any way, you will never again think of yourself as not good enough or unworthy or incapable. You will be free to be proud of who you really are as a human being.

This is the first and most important step in changing your life for the better - accepting there is nothing wrong with you as a human being. Therefore, you should never be ashamed of yourself as a person. Of course, we all make mistakes and poor choices as we grow but this is a part of the natural and necessary process for learning and growth.

Because you were born perfect, you can never be a bad person. Because you have "free will," you certainly can make bad or poor choices but bad choices in themselves do not make you a bad person. There is a real difference.

The term *"free will"* refers to the universal need for everyone to make choices for themselves. We all have a need for freedom and independence which is evident every day in people's ongoing resistance to being dominated or controlled. It is the concept of "free will" which makes choices possible in order for the world to continually evolve to a better place.

If you didn't have "free will", then something outside you would be controlling you and you would never want to be controlled ... would you?

As you grew up, you may have found yourself in circumstances tempting you to make choices you didn't realize were ultimately wrong for both you and those around you. However, you must always remember a bad choice does not make you a bad person or change the person you really are. As you will see later, a bad choice is usually a combination of factors resulting from false information you believed to be the truth.

Although you were born as a perfect human being, your childhood experiences, which were not perfect, began to influence and shape the way you think, feel and behave. These experiences were not chosen by you but rather by parents, family members and those surrounding you during your dependent years. All these people had their own beliefs and biases they attempted to instill within you. You were very young and without the ability to understand how and why things were happening the way they did. Often, your only understanding was in the form of feelings – either good or bad. Your very early responses could only be either a smile or a cry.

Today, an important step in your adulthood is for you to recognize that past beliefs formed and earlier experiences are actually in the past and not in your present or future unless you allow them to be there. As an adult you would be wise to question the truth of your beliefs as you continue your life journey. Throughout your life, your past experiences should not be forgotten or repressed, but rather remain as a part of your memory and used as important lessons learned.

Being a sensible person with free will, you cannot allow unpleasant feelings from the past to become so powerful they turn into the dominant factors driving your present life and future path.

Bad experiences from the past are often powerful factors causing pain and torment when we bring them into our daily lives. Bad experiences can disrupt and destroy our present and future prospects for greater success and happiness. But that is the case only if you choose to allow them to torment you. Since you have "free will" they have no power without your consent.

In the following chapters, we will discuss the process for you to use to replace all your false beliefs with the truth. For now, accept you have some false beliefs about yourself from the past and promise yourself to always remain open to replacing them with real truths as they appear.

Also, remember that because you were given "free will" at birth (although it was not possible for you to fully use before adulthood), the choice is always yours regarding your actions, beliefs, and decisions.

SO, What Is The Wisdom In This Chapter and … What Do You Do With This Information?

Be proud of who you are as a human being … forever.

Accept that you were born a precious and perfect human being and you can never change what God and Mother Nature created (You).

Acknowledge and correct any mistakes you may make but never be ashamed of whom you really are as a human being. This is one of the most important realities you must accept.

Recognize experiences in your early life formed your beliefs about yourself. Those beliefs need to be questioned by you as an adult because they may not all be true and "false beliefs" can lead you to repeated wrong decisions.

Accept that making mistakes are a natural part of learning and what you did does not reflect who you are as a person.

Because you were born with "free will," choices are always yours.

Your childhood experiences are in the past (gone forever) and can never be in your present or future unless you allow them in.

Never think of yourself as broken, damaged or defeated—only perhaps unwilling.

Before we go on to Chapter Three, you should take the time to understand the wisdom and guidance in this chapter. Who you honestly believe you are is central to what you think you can do and what you will actually achieve for yourself. Later in this book, I will help you to learn how to trust yourself rather than rely on others, so you can always maintain the "real truth" about you. If you still refuse to believe in yourself based on your creation, then you should pause and take the time to reconsider the thoughts I shared with you. However, if you are willing to continue to explore and expose your inner secrets to yourself, see the truth and can now accept you were born and remain a perfect human being, then you already made tremendous progress toward your future growth and happiness.

Remember that all your choices and actions in your life could never be perfect, but your original creation was perfect and this can never change. At this point, you may have already reduced your urge to shoplift or "act out" in some way because you know this is not who you truly are and realize you have the ability to replace one behavior for another if you wish to do so.

If you now feel more confident about yourself, read on.

Note: To help you gauge the value of the words in this book, you may turn to Appendix III for a sample of the comments from people who shoplifted and received private Telephone Coaching sessions with the author. Their own words may bring you a clearer understanding.

CHAPTER 3

Life Throws Us Curves

Your Response Is What Makes The Difference

To demonstrate how people deal with life's trials and tribulations, I thought it best to share examples from my own life. The curves or curveballs thrown at me in my life might help you in dealing with the curves life through your way. With that said, one of the more significant curveballs I experienced was when I was fifty years old, after my parents had passed away, I accidentally found out I was adopted. Naturally, I was shocked and thought to myself, "WOW."

At first I said, "There must be some mistake. I would have known about this. It simply can't be true." After pausing for a moment to truly evaluate this unbelievable news, I thought to myself, "what if it is true?" Wild thoughts ran through my mind and unusual sensations surfaced for the first time. Underlying emotions I always denied suddenly began to make sense. Now it seemed clear why some family members seemed so distant from me. I couldn't believe it. As I looked at the evidence, I began to accept it might be true that "my parents" were not my birth parents or even related by blood.

I felt that for 50 years I was deceived. I don't know why my parents and other family members didn't tell me I was adopted, but I can only imagine my adopted parents were afraid I might feel or do something hurtful to myself or to them. Unfortunately, as I began to make further inquiries I discovered this was one of many deceptions that would be revealed about my life.

This discovery would be a shock for anyone. However, depending upon the type of person you are, shattering news like this could carry a wide range of affects on you. Like almost all situations in your life, it depends on whether you can step outside of your emotions long enough so that you can objectively see the real truth surrounding your own situation. Many people eagerly asked me "How did you find out?"

I never would have found out I was adopted if my daughter wasn't going to have a baby. I had always been told that I had a brother who died six months before I was born from Taysachs, a hereditary disease. Thus, my daughter's doctor insisted she be tested for this genetic disorder, as it was expected it had passed through the generations. When the test results came back from the lab, it revealed my daughter did not have the gene for Taysachs, which meant that I didn't have the gene. I asked, "How could this be correct?" The doctor indicated the result could not be correct unless I was adopted. "What a ridiculous notion", I spouted out.

After months of prodding by my daughter to confirm if I was adopted, I reluctantly contacted the State of New York. The answer came back that I was adopted. The State indicated my birth mother was unwed and could not afford to care for me, a common scenario in Brooklyn in the 1940's. "Unbelievable," I shouted.

I had no one to ask questions regarding my adoption because almost everyone in my family had already died, except an uncle and some younger cousins. I was raised as an only child and my mother died when I was fifteen and my father died when I was thirty-five.

When it was confirmed, many thoughts went through my mind. First, I still denied such a thing was even possible. Then, instead of feeling grateful to my adopted parents for raising me, I felt angry about this deceit because I eventually learned everyone knew the truth except me. I began to think about the reasons my birth mother gave me up; whether my birth parents were alive; whether I had any living siblings; and numerous questions about my heritage and hereditary health.

Weeks later, I invited an uncle I had not seen for years to come for dinner. Having suspected I found out about my adoption, he brought with him a court paper showing proof of my adoption and my original birth name, David Herdt. He never revealed this to me before because he had promised my mother to keep this secret. Fortunately, he was able to fill-in a few of the blanks about my past, even though he was overseas in the British Navy during WW II when I was born.

As the story unfolded, it appeared my parents took me in when I was one year old but officially adopted me when I was about 1 ½ years old.

No one knew where I was placed during that first year. I don't know if I was in a foster home, an orphanage, several foster homes or whatever?

Because both my parents were teachers, I was raised largely by a Nanny. My mother was not around very much because she left the house at 7:00 AM for work in the Bronx and didn't return home to Brooklyn until almost 6:00 PM. For as long as I can remember, my mother always seemed distant and not as warm and loving as other mothers appeared to be. Years later I realized that my mother never bonded with me as a child, creating a situation where I always hungered for her love. My father was a loving man but was always busy.

The questions on my mind ranged from: why did my birth mother really give me up for adoption after carrying me for nine months to why did my adopted mother not bond with me if she chose to adopt me? Regrettably, I never found the answers to these questions.

At first, after hearing what my uncle had to say, I felt angry at everyone about being abandoned and deceived. Of course, I was only thinking about myself. I would ask myself "why me?" It felt as if something must be wrong with me. Later, I began to realize I was not the only one involved. I realized what happened to me really had nothing to do with me and was not the result of anything I did or didn't do, but rather was a result of the actions and decisions of other people. In reality, I was simply in that place at that moment in time, not because there was something wrong with me or because someone was trying to hurt me. However, it became apparent that some negative feelings I had developed about myself in my early years were certainly the result of the circumstances surrounding my birth and my adoption.

As I searched for the truth, I concluded it is a fair assumption a birth mother would not want to give up her baby because it was normally a very difficult thing for a mother to do. Therefore, because she did give me up for adoption, there had to be a darn good reason. It certainly could not have had anything to do with me. I was an infant. The reason had to hinge around the circumstances surrounding my birth mother's life at the time. She may have been unwed, poor, or handicapped. My uncle told me he heard my birth mother petitioned the court to get me back in later years but the court said "No" because the adoption was finalized.

I started putting the pieces together, trying to come to terms with everything so this curve thrown my way would not overwhelm my emotions or derail my life going forward. As I thought about my adopted mother, I tried to understand why she didn't bond with me and why she could not love me. Whatever the reason, I came to the conclusion it was not my fault. Then it hit me.

First of all, it definitely could not have been because of me because, clearly, I was too cute. Secondly, I remembered that my brother who was the natural child of my adopted parents had died an agonizing death from Taysachs at age three, just six months or so before my parents adopted me. I was told children with Taysachs are born normally but then slowly deteriorate by losing muscle coordination and experiencing seizures, paralysis, deafness, blindness, all resulting in a premature death in the first few years of life. I can only imagine that after he died, my mother must have been so distraught and depressed about his illness and death that her family probably urged her in a caring way to "get another puppy" so to speak, so she could move on with her life. So I believe she got another puppy - Me.

Unfortunately, it didn't work. My mother turned to her career as a school teacher rather than to her family. I will never know the ultimate affects of her tragic loss, but there is a good possibility no matter how hard she tried, she wasn't able to love me after the loss of her son. Or perhaps, she was too afraid to love another son for fear she might somehow lose me too, a loss she could never endure again. While I will never know the truth, I do believe it was nobody's fault. It was the circumstances at the time. Even though I was hurt as a result of my mother's estrangement, I believe the truth is nobody was trying to hurt me.

Therefore, there was no blame. And if there is no blame, there is certainly no anger because anger comes from blame. It is now possible for me to understand, forgive and accept what appears most probably to be the truth. If I chose to believe and hold onto a more negative version of this experience, it would only serve my own self-centered feelings, and make me feel like a victim and promote a perpetual state of anger and entitlement. Since it is solely my choice regarding what to believe in the absence of positive proof, I decided to accept the story that sounded most like the real truth and made the most sense to me. I never wanted to deceive myself. Because of this choice, I feel at peace. Basically, I decided it was wrong to blame anybody and there was no justifiable reason to feel like a victim or carry anger towards anyone.

The Next Curve

The next upheaval in my early life started when I was four years old. At that time, my parents moved into different bedrooms and were divorced by the time I was six. For me, this was more traumatic than anything before, probably because I was older and more aware. Because their divorce occurred in the 1940's when none of my friends had divorced parents, I was especially devastated. Again, I was being hurt by the loss of parents but in reality I later recognized the hurt was not directed towards me. I was not the cause of the divorce, just an innocent bystander. If anything, the fact they adopted a child probably prolonged their separation.

As a child, the divorce was very difficult for me. I refused to accept what I saw as the loss of my parents and family. I fought the divorce in every way imaginable. In the beginning, at age six, when I was with my father on the way to the courthouse for a custody hearing, my father asked me to tell the judge I wanted to live with him rather than my mother. When it came time to speak, I told the judge at the custody hearing that if I couldn't live with both my parents I refused to live with either of them. I seemingly tried to "take charge" because I felt both my parents were "out of control." While custody was ultimately given to my mother, I would never accept her or my father dating another person. So much so,

I did whatever I could to sabotage any new relationship they tried to develop.

Once, my father came to my house and my mother's boyfriend was there. The boyfriend told me to "shut up" in front of my father and the two men starting fist fighting in my living room which was certainly traumatic for me.

After five long years of divorce, when I was eleven years old, my mother and father got remarried … yes, to one another, and I was at the ceremony. Honestly, how many people can say they were at their parent's wedding? I saw them kiss on the alter and it was my happiest moment. I dreamed of our future together, buying a new home in Whitestone, New York, and being a family again.

Unfortunately, my mother was soon diagnosed with colon cancer and died within two years. A year after her death, my father remarried and I was sent away to military school. After fighting so long to regain my family, I lost them again, this time forever.

Another Curve

Another curveball in the saga of my life came years later when I thought I found my birth mother. However, she rejected the fact I was her son. A friend saw a newspaper article about a memorial service for a man with my original birth name who lived in a nearby town. My wife and I decided to attend the service and quietly learned some facts about his life. As the story goes, at the time I was born, the man was married but separated from his wife. He was seeing a graduate college student whom he later married as his second wife. As the facts came together, I believe he had an affair with a college student who became pregnant. Being unmarried and financially unable to support a child, she put the child up for adoption. Remember that in the 1940's it was very shameful to have a child out of wedlock.

About a month after the memorial service, my wife and I went to visit his widow and from the moment we saw her we knew she was my mother. We looked so much alike. While I had little doubt she was my mother, she insisted she never had a child before marriage and that I was not her son. I suspect she reacted this way because she felt she didn't want to reveal her earlier indiscretion to her other children or tarnish her upstanding reputation as a college professor. Or perhaps, she may have suspected my appearance at this opportune time was simply to become eligible for a part of her considerable estate.

While I was certainly overcome with disappointment, whatever her reasons, I decided not to pursue it any further and allow her to keep her deep secret. While it was difficult for me to think my own mother would not want to acknowledge her son, I understood her feelings were no less important than mine. That is why I respected her decision and never reached out to her again.

As I reflect today, I believe the loss of my birth mother, the loss of my foster parents, my adopted mother's withdrawal from me, and my parents' divorce had a profound influence on my early life and my future. At age sixteen, with my yearning for love and family, I met Meryl, a girl of fourteen who was so sweet, accepting and non-judgmental that I attached myself to her immediately. As we dated, after only about four months, I felt she was the girl for me because I somehow knew she would be loyal and would never leave me. I needed to know this because subconsciously I felt I could never endure a divorce or suffer the loss of any more loved ones in my life.

After a five and one-half year relationship, I married Meryl. She was nineteen and I was twenty-one. In truth, simply by loving me deeply, Meryl undoubtedly saved my life from "God knows what," because I was an unhappy person and her loving me always made me feel I was a better man than I thought I was. We eventually had two children and have now been married 49 years and counting.

With all that happened, somehow my parent's divorce was, and remains, the most traumatic experience of my life. Although I know divorce is far more common today, I also know its effects can still be enormously damaging.

SO, What Is The Wisdom In This Chapter and ... What Do You Do With This Information?

When life throws you curves, it is not the other person's actions but rather your response to those actions that will determine your future.

Self-defeating behaviors develop when there is a false interpretation of the truth which leads one to accept a false impression of self.

I have told you my story because everyone's experiences in the beginning of life were very different, some better and some worse. Regardless, *it was what it was.* The only thing you can do about it today is to understand and accept these truths:

You were born perfect, precious and innocent just as God and Mother Nature intended you to be.

You must never blame yourself for things which occurred during your earlier innocence.

Things that happened to you were not your fault.

You were not the cause of the hurts you experienced as you grew up.

You should not blame others who hurt you because their intent was not to hurt you but rather to satisfy their own needs or issues. This may have been misguided on their part, perhaps because they were dysfunctional in some way.

To replace your hurt emotions with understanding based on your own wisdom and belief of what was probably the truth at the time ... and to wisely use the lessons it taught.

Remember, scars are a symbol of the past, not a predictor of the future.

As an adult, go forward today by releasing your past blame of others and replace your hurt feelings with what you have come to believe is a more realistic and sensible version of the truth at the time. When others don't meet your expectations today, don't choose to blame others and then feel like a victim. Rather, look at what you did or didn't do to alter the situation. Maybe you just put your trust in the wrong person. This way of responding makes great sense to me and I hope to you. Keep going forward.

If you don't choose to go forward, you will always remain in the same place or begin to slide backward. Remember, your future starts now, not tomorrow.

CHAPTER 4

What Are The Things You Really Need In Your Life?

Self-defeating behaviors develop when one feels confused and unable to identify and satisfy their fundamental human needs and seeks alternatives in a self-defeating way.

Whether you are a man or a woman, we all have the same primary emotional needs. We all desire to feel safe, loved, and free from control, while simultaneously feeling good about ourselves. There are also primary physical needs requiring our attention. Physically, we all have to breathe, to eat and go to the bathroom. Preserving life and seeking satisfaction of our primary needs motivate us on a daily basis.

This chapter is about identifying and understanding the areas in life you need to maintain in order to feel settled and satisfied. I tell you this because when any of your basic human needs are threatened and you feel fearful, depressed, or dissatisfied, you may tend to seek satisfaction or relief elsewhere, sometimes in a negative manner. Whether it is in the form of alcohol, drugs, overeating, anorexia, self-mutilation, shoplifting, compulsive shopping, gambling or any other self-defeating behavior, these actions may be temporarily self-satisfying but are almost always self-destructive.

Before I discuss in more detail about our primary human needs, let me first offer you a simple framework for your life.

Health — Work — Relationships

Everything we have to be concerned about in this world can be summed up into three broad categories of life. These are Health, Work, and Relationships.

Everything that means anything to you can be accomplished by maintaining your health, working to satisfy many needs of life, and by maintaining good relationships with people - especially that one person who is your partner in life. Thus, the focus and energy in your life should be on these three things.

For example, to accomplish anything for yourself or others, you need your health. To fulfill your responsibilities for yourself and your family, you need to make personal accomplishments and money, which is simply a natural consequence of what you do eight hours a day – work. To satisfy your emotional needs for yourself and your family, you must maintain good relationships with others inside and outside of your home.

It is doubtful you can think of anything that isn't covered within the three categories of Health, Work and Relationships.

Does anything else come to mind for you?

If not, it shouldn't be a problem to accept these as the three categories where you need to maintain stability in your life. As you move forward, keep these three categories in mind rather than worrying about anything else. This idea should make your life less complicated because it is only three things.

With that said, what does all this have to do with shoplifting or other self-defeating behaviors?

Shoplifting and other self-defeating behaviors are only a "symptom" or "signal" of an underlying inner problem and is largely a reflection of a person's ability or inability to cope with issues in their life. If that person uses only these three categories to uncomplicate his or her life, he or she can then cure the fundamental problem as well. In order to remove the stress, frustrations, anxiety, depression, feelings of anger, guilt, shame, and entitlement that can lead to different types of self-defeating behaviors, you should understand that your life is not as complicated as it may appear and accept that these three categories of your life are manageable for you.

Although it may seem obvious, let us take a little closer look to help clarify your understanding of these three categories:

Health

Your health is most important. When you are young and generally in good health, it carries little meaning and you rarely focus time and attention on it. However, as you age or your health takes a turn for the worse, you have no choice because your health suddenly demands your almost complete focus because all other things become immediately compromised. Health is certainly everyone's number one.

If you are in good health now, simply be aware of how important good health is and do as much as you wish to preserve it.

However, if you are not in good health due to one or more health issues, view your situation in realistic terms, particularly with regard to whether your condition is temporary or permanent. Whatever the circumstances, be sure to continue working to improve your condition and/or decide how you will continue to enjoy your life in spite of your issues. While a chronic illness is always sad, any choice you make that is not realistic can only be self-defeating and insure further unhappiness.

Even with poor health circumstances, it would be related to a miracle if you could inspire yourself to work as one of those people who have lifted themselves up from being a victim to being admired.

Work

The sun rises and sets every day of your life and what you do to fill up those eight plus (8+) hours a day has enormous implications on your life.

Whether you are a stay at home mom, you go to a structured job assignment, or you are an entrepreneur, your job offers the opportunity to experience the personal satisfaction (and money) you need to survive. For example:

- Doing your job well can give you special recognition, a feeling of pride and self-worth.
- How well you perform your job gives you opportunities for advancement.
- What you do determines how you contribute to your world and/or how much money you earn.
- Being free to make decisions develops your creativity and self-worth.
- Meeting others can lead to important work friendships.
- Meeting others can lead to love relationships.
- Working with others gives you a better sense of who you are in relation to others.

What you choose to do and how you choose to do it will help you develop a satisfying (or dissatisfying) sense of yourself that can uplift (or bring down) your spirit every day. You have a choice to begin each day of your life looking to conquer the unknown challenges ahead or begin feeling pessimistic and unsuccessful. You can try to achieve something or try to avoid something. Regardless of what you choose, the choice is always yours and most probably within your reach.

Regardless of your current work situation, don't allow temporary setbacks to keep you from moving forward. If you do, you will damage the future for yourself and the ones you love.

Even if you feel down from all the hurdles and struggles you faced, until you can get things on track, grit your teeth and *"suffer like an adult"* until you work things out … which, if you keep putting one foot in front of the other, you clearly will.

Relationships

Relationships are often the most difficult of the three categories in which to find ongoing satisfaction.

My forty-nine-year relationship with my wife has clearly been the most difficult relationship I've ever had, but it has also been my most rewarding relationship.

You already know the importance of relationships in your life. While relationships are the subject of many books, I will address a few important truths regarding maintaining relationships that may help you reduce unrealistic expectations of people and gain a better perspective on your own relationship. Disappointments in relationships can lead to self-defeating behaviors by causing you to accept blame, guilt or by feeling like a victim.

(Don't lose sight of the fact that all this is connected to self-defeating behaviors.)

Insights Into the Dynamics of Relationships

First, recognize your relationships with people are on many different levels because you play many different roles in both their lives and yours.

At different times you are a child, teenager, grown son or daughter, sibling, friend, student, team member, boyfriend or girlfriend, employee, co-worker, supervisor, patient, client, spouse, partner, parent, grandparent, uncle or aunt, community leader, volunteer, public servant, and many more roles.

It would be unrealistic for you to believe you could play all roles equally well throughout life. This is one reason why the most successful couples choose partners who can compliment (not duplicate) their strengths and weaknesses. Ultimately, you can only do what you believe to be your best while not compromising your true self.

Second, each role you play requires a different type of focus and often a different level of understanding. You think differently as a child vs. parent, a worker vs. supervisor, a girlfriend vs. spouse, a sister vs. friend, or a citizen vs. a public servant. Recognize you will think and act differently when you are in different roles and have different responsibilities. Give those in opposite roles the same consideration you would ask for yourself. Don't expect to have the same perspective when you are performing in different roles and make sure to be clear about who you are in your current role to avoid misunderstanding.

Third, the other person in any relationship with you was born with different genetics, raised by different parents, had different family members and friends, received different schooling and experienced life differently than you. Thus, that person will always be similar but also different than you in many important ways. Maintaining a good relationship with any person on various levels requires two people to be in harmony in many similar ways.

This is not easy. Don't allow yourself to become easily disappointed because you expect people to act and think as you would. Try not to be judgmental and simply allow others to be who they are and you be who you are. Due to this fact, you can definitely expect to have hundreds of casual relationships in your life, with only a select few of them turning into close friendships because of the natural differences between people.

Forth, realize you can have a good relationship with people on a few levels, but not on all levels. Realize this so your expectations are not so high as to cause unnecessary personal disappointment for you. For example, you can go out to dinner with one couple as long as you don't discuss politics; you can have a barbecue at another couple's house but you can't play cards with them because they are too competitive; you can go shopping with a girlfriend but you may not be able to double-date because your girlfriend is a very jealous person. Almost all relationships carry restrictions and you would be wise to realize what kind of a relationship you can or can't have with those you befriend. If you decide to maintain a relationship with someone in spite of your differences, don't try to simply tolerate their behavior but rather accept it as part of who they are, even though you may not agree with it.

Due to all these uncontrollable variables in life, you can't expect to play these different roles perfectly. However, you need to do your best without sacrificing your dignity or being unfair to either yourself or others.

Don't allow yourself to become unhappy because of these simple life realities and never demand more than another person can possibly give.

Of course, relatives are different. You didn't pick them and they didn't pick you ... especially your in-laws. However, it is wise to give relatives greater acceptance and more latitude to make mistakes without immediate outrage or repercussions. While some retort can be tempting, your best move will always be to resolve disharmony. They have a responsibility to be nice too but you can only control your behavior, not theirs. All you can do is respond to their actions in the manner you feel is proper and in accordance with your values.

If they are unresponsive, then you may have to move away from such encounters but if possible, always leave the door open.

Four Fundamental Human Needs Which We All Must Continuously Satisfy

It is nice to know that there are only three broad categories that need your attention to simplify your life. However, to be able to function effectively within these categories, you first have to clear away any threat to the four fundamental human needs existing in all of us.

These fundamental human needs are:

- Your need for Security – being safe from physical harm.
- Your need for Love – being loved and loving others.
- Your need for Freedom and Independence – being free, not controlled.
- Your need for Self-Worth – being useful, worthwhile, feeling good about self.

On any given day, should you find yourself feeling frightened, anxious, depressed, dysfunctional, preoccupied or some other unsettled feeling, it is almost always a signal to you that one of your four fundamental needs are being threatened. Your primary attention will then always be directed to removing the threat.

For example, if your boss is too demanding, this can cause you to worry about your job security. If your spouse is unhappy, this can cause you to worry about your love relationship. If your spouse is controlling, this can cause you to feel that you lost your independence or freedom. If you begin to experience criticism from others, you may stop feeling good about yourself and start to question your own self-worth.

Please don't doubt or deny you have these needs because your denial will not make them go away. Rather than denial, embrace these four fundamental needs as part of your humanity. Whenever you can see which of your four needs is being threatened, you will then beome more capable of responding to remove the threat.

This is an enormously helpful way to cope if you fully understand its power.

It simplifies your problems and points you to a quicker solution. To help you see the importance of these fundamental needs, consider below common examples of possible threats to your needs and consider why you will always remain anxious and unsettled when you feel any one of your four fundamental needs are threatened.

By looking at the examples, you will see how you can become pre-occupied (and partly dysfunctional) until these threats are eliminated.

Security:

You will remain anxious and unsettled if your parents are going to get a divorce and you do not know what is going to happen to you. When you learn you are not going to lose the love and support of your parents, the threat to your security will be gone. You will remain anxious and unsettled if you feel your physical safety is in danger for any reason. When your fear of a bully who threatened to beat you up, a criminal who threatened to kill you, a drunken or angry father, a jealous husband or other such thing is gone, the threat to your security would disappear with these scenarios.

You will remain anxious and unsettled if you feel insecure due to a physical handicap. When you are given assistance or learn how to care for yourself, the threat to your security would be gone.

You will remain anxious and unsettled if you lost your job. When you got a new job, the immediate threat to your security would be gone.

Love

You will remain anxious and unsettled if you feel unloved by your spouse or partner. When you find love again with your spouse or move on to another partner, your need for love will be resolved.

You will remain anxious and unsettled if you feel important people in your life do not desire, want, accept, admire or appreciate you. When you ultimately realize these people do either desire, want, accept, admire and/ or appreciate you in some ways, but not in all ways, the threat to your not feeling loved or accepted will be resolved.

You will remain anxious and unsettled if you are unhappy in your marriage. When you and your partner originally decided to make a commitment, love was an important part of the reason. Expectations were that both of you would contribute equally to the relationship by fulfilling your respective roles. If you and your spouse are able to make preserving your original marriage relationship the top priority, the importance of the love relationship will feel evident, rather than engaging in the unhealthy practice of getting what one wants at the expense of the other. When this shift occurs, the threat to your marriage will probably be eliminated. In addition, if you want to take care of your children, first take care of your love relationship with your spouse and the threat to your children (and you) will be gone.

Freedom and Independence

You will remain anxious and unsettled if you feel someone or something is trying to control your spending.

You will remain anxious and unsettled if you feel you do not have free will to choose your own path.

When it comes down to it, all living things instinctively resist control because it restricts the evolution of life. To avoid feeling anxious or unsettled, don't try to control any living thing or restrict *free will,* as most human beings will resist anything that tries to control them.

The best and most lasting way to get what you want is to be in harmony with others rather than try and force things upon them.

Self-Worth

You will remain anxious and unsettled if you falsely believe you are not a worthwhile person. For example, if you believe that your parents do not love or value you as a person as much as other parents.

You will remain anxious and unsettled if you do not feel you can hold your head up and feel proud of yourself.

Regardless of whom you are, the things causing you to feel unworthy as a person came from your interaction with others and are almost always false beliefs on your part. Other people may believe you are unworthy in some manner but you should always know that is not the real truth. As you read earlier, you were born as a perfect human being and can never be imperfect or unworthy. At times, your actions may be misguided, but this is all part of the learning experience.

When this happens, take responsibility for your behavior and then simply move on without blame, anger, guilt or shame.

If you think about it, it is precisely your feelings of guilt, shame and regret which clearly proves your good intentions and worthiness.

Your recognition of your true worth is absolutely essential to your well-being and happiness. If you do not see yourself as being the person you want to be, keep trying until you see it because inevitably you will.

(Don't lose sight of the fact that all this is connected to self-defeating behaviors.)

Who Comes First?

A vital part of your fundamental need for safety and security is to sustain your life. What this also means to you is that *you come first.*

Always putting yourself first is not suggesting selfish behavior, but rather, a practical reality. Here is a common example showing why you must come first. When you are on any airplane and you see the safety message about using the oxygen mask if there is a loss of cabin pressure, the safety film always shows an adult sitting next to a child.

The announcement then indicates you should place an oxygen mask on yourself then the child. Why? If you pass out, who is going to help the child? This example is a life lesson teaching you that while the child is dependent on you, if you don't put yourself first, you may not be in a position to help others. Satisfying all your basic needs requires that you put yourself before everyone and everything else.

Let's consider another example about putting yourself first, this time related to the need for love. Think about your answer to the following question: why did you marry your husband or wife? Was it for your benefit or the benefit of your spouse?

For me, the simple truth is I wanted the love of a woman and she wanted the love of a man. I married my wife because I thought she could make me happy and care for me and she did exactly the same thing. Why I chose one woman over another is a different issue. No one, except an unstable person, would make a life commitment without expecting something in return. Is this selfish? Not at all! Any other type relationship would be grossly unfair to one or the other partner. The partner receiving less than they gave would eventually feel cheated, resentful, dissatisfied and inevitably lose interest in continuing the relationship on the same basis. You may love a person forever but if he or she does not fairly uphold his or her end of the partnership responsibilities, the relationship will eventually crumble.

Relationships will never be exactly equal in regard to what one partner does for the other but there is the need for balance and to feel your partner is contributing to the relationship in a manner which makes it fair and worthwhile for you. One partner can make a home and raise the children while the other takes responsibility for the financial welfare of the family. It doesn't matter who does what, but it just needs to be reasonably balanced. Of course, if one partner later becomes disabled in some way, then as long as the one disabled does the best he or she can, that is all anyone can ask and the love and respect in the relationship would help the relationship to survive.

Does this reasoning really support why everyone must take care of one's self first? Absolutely! Is it selfish? Absolutely Not! I think you would agree it is exactly the way it should be, that is basically fair or at least satisfying to both partners throughout the entire lifetime of the relationship. It is not ok to slack off after 30 years.

I always realized that my wife's love, while loyal, was also somewhat conditional in the sense the relationship would begin to dissolve if she were unhappy. That is why I have learned (sometimes painfully) what I must do to keep her happy and satisfied – for ME.

Defining Priorities

My first obligation is to take care of me so I am able to contribute to the family and never become a burden to my spouse and children. So, my first obligation to my loved ones is to take care of me.

My second obligation is to maintain a healthy relationship with my spouse so the relationship does not fall apart and my children do not suffer the loss of a mom or dad. By the standards of any child, the most important thing a dad can do for his children is to love their mother and vice-versa. In the best of situations, both parents are needed to properly raise a child because each parent offers a balance every child needs.

My third obligation is to care for my child. However, if I take care of myself and my partner, I already did my job of caring for my child. After all, if both parents are well and capable, what does the child have to worry about? He or she will almost always be protected and cared for. However, if one parent is missing in the home, it is frequently much more difficult to care for a child—both physically, financially and emotionally.

Of course, there can be rare times when caring for your child can become a higher priority over your spouse. This can happen when one spouse continually does not hold up his or her end of the bargain. In such instance, you must use your best judgment while encouraging your spouse to focus on the value of maintaining the love relationship rather than the value of *anything else.*

It is important to realize the man is one entity, the woman is another entity and the relationship is a different entity. After a man and woman marry, a new third entity is established called the 'relationship'. We all have different likes and dislikes as well as various ideas about things, but the purpose of any marriage is to focus on maintaining the established relationship. The words "you" and "me" must now take a back seat to the word "us."

Putting yourself first does not mean satisfying your own whims before everything else. It simply means not allowing your physical or emotional health to deteriorate to a point where you become a burden to either yourself or others. You must always remain sound. There is no limit to the things you can choose to do for others but remember it is always your choice. No one has a right to your life. Your life is sacred beyond all others, a notion recognized in the laws of all nations. That's why the only acceptable reason for killing another human being is self-defense (i.e. your life comes first.)

The important point to remember is not to allow your elderly parents, your children, your job or your extended family to demand or consume so much of your time that you become burned-out or ill. You must remember to keep your priorities straight and never sacrifice one of your priorities for another. Keep it all balanced and intact.

When my father became partially senile and too old to care for himself, it made me sad to place him in a home other than my own. However, it would have been too much of a strain on my family to have him live with us. Had I lived alone, my father would have certainly lived with me. My priority was clear.

Balancing all parts of your life so you can remain a well functioning human being is imperative to your personal success. The thing to remember is you have a deep responsibility to many things and being responsible means remaining balanced and not allowing yourself to sacrifice any one of your top priorities for another.

People cannot rightfully take your physical life or quality of life without your consent. You can choose to throw yourself in front of a passing train to save a child if you wish but that is your choice. No one has the right to expect you to give up your life unless you choose to. In addition, no one is able to force you to sacrifice your quality of life, unless you have somehow forfeited this right. Of course, if you committed a crime, you may be forced to forfeit your right to freedom while in prison. But other than something like this, the choice remains with you.

Take care of yourself first because this is the only way to care for others as well. Don't let anything or anyone put you in second place, without your consent. Don't ever allow yourself to feel guilty or unworthy because of other's beliefs. No one has the right or ability to control you without your consent. The choice is always yours. They cannot remove your choice but they can sometimes make your choices more difficult and that's what they refer to as 'difficult choices'.

We all have the right to our own freedom and we have to continually assert ourselves in various ways to retain that freedom and independence throughout our lifetime or we will lose it.

SO, What Is The Wisdom In This Chapter and ... What Do You Do With This Information?

Your life need not be so complicated.

Simplify your focus in life: Health, Work, and Relationships.

Remember, you have four fundamental needs whenever you feel stress or feel unsettled: Need for Security/Safety, Love, Freedom / Independence and Self-Worth. Be aware whenever you feel one or more of these four fundamental needs are being threatened. Therefore, whenever you feel frightened, anxious, depressed, dysfunctional, preoccupied or in some other way unsettled, identify which of your needs are being threatened and see what action(s) would be required by you to remove that threat. Then, do what you must in a lawful and responsible manner.

Remember you are not a victim but rather a capable human being who has responsibility for your own life.

Know your priorities: Yourself, your spouse, your children, your livelihood, your parents, your in-laws, your close relatives, real friends and others who may be very special. One of the most important priorities is the love 'relationship' with your spouse because that is the cement that can hold everything together.

Take care of yourself first so you are capable of caring for your loved ones. Don't sacrifice yourself, or allow the pressures to build inside you to a point where you begin to become dysfunctional. This is your life and you only have one – so make sure you are in charge of it.

(Don't lose sight of the fact that all this is connected to self-defeating behaviors.)

CHAPTER 5

Who and What Can You Trust?

Self-defeating behaviors often develop as a response to a lack of trust in other alternatives available.

Without trust you cannot move forward. Therefore, let us understand the importance of trust and how we can learn to trust in order to avoid the unpleasant consequences of engaging in self-defeating behaviors.

Trust is something we all rely upon every hour of every day. It is vital to your development that you are comfortable with the decisions you make. Making any decision always involves trust because you have to believe you are going to be safe.

How you trust others and how others trust you dramatically shapes your life by either allowing things to move forward or causing things to step back.

Every day you unknowingly decide to trust many different things. However, you are probably not aware of how important your trust is to you. For example, you trust the food you are eating is not spoiled or poisoned and the company who prepared and delivered that same food took the necessary precautions to ensure the safety of its customers. You trust the car driver coming toward you in the opposite direction will stay on his side of the white line; you trust the school teacher to take care of your child; the mechanic to put the right parts in your car; the doctor to properly diagnose and treat you; the pharmacist to fill the right prescription; the electrician to properly wire your home; a friend not to lie to you; and you especially want to trust the person who says "I love you."

While I suspect you are reading this book because you hope my words will guide you to a better place in life, the best way for you to ensure your safety is to *trust yourself.* You must always be your own person.

This means you must put your trust in your own judgment and feelings, not the judgment of others. In life, you must commit to always taking full responsibility for yourself including making your own decisions. This is the *only way* you will have the personal freedom you desire and be the person you want to be in all situations in your life.

Marcus Garvey, a Jamaican publisher, entrepreneur, and orator once said,

"If you have no confidence in self, you are twice defeated in the race for life. With confidence, you have won even before you have started."

It is only your own judgment and feelings you should trust even if you don't know or are unsure of the answer to many of your questions. Even though you might like to rely on others for a solution, you really never know whether you can trust the guidance of others because people have their own opinions, ideas and prejudices. Certain people may sincerely think they are giving you the proper advice but it is you who must decide if the advice feels right for you.

In truth, when you choose to put your trust in someone or something, it is really not that person or object you are trusting. What you are really trusting is your belief in your own judgment about whether that person or object is trustworthy.

So, if what I write and the way I write it is something you choose to believe, then what you should be relying on is whether my words and thoughts agree with your own sense of what is right or wrong for you. Only then can you begin to accept some of my thoughts as your own. If in the future, you decide to follow someone's advice and it later proves to be wrong for you, then you should not find comfort in blaming that other person but rather examining your own judgment leading to your trust. Trust is always your decision and responsibility.

Trust is not something you can blindly give to others. It is one of the most precious freedoms you have and you should forever examine your trust decisions to continually protect and strengthen its ability to help you make better choices for you. In my experience, the ability to know how and when to trust came to you from God or Mother Nature at birth. When you were born you were given the power to see the truth in the form of feelings. This is largely how a jury in a murder case can reach decisions about life or death without having direct knowledge of what really happened. It is your feelings and innate wisdom which tells you if something feels good or not to you. Even babies innately know to cry when they hear a loud noise or smile when they see a happy face.

Even in those cases where you must put your trust in another person, such as a surgeon, what you really should be trusting is your own understanding of your condition, the doctor's medical credentials, hospital affiliations, reputation, the feeling of trust you have in the person referring you to the doctor and your feelings from the personal consultation you had in his office. Except in a dire emergency, trust is not something you can blindly afford to give to others just because you feel unsure or are too lazy to protect yourself by connecting with your own feelings. If you don't use your ability, then you are doomed to accept whatever you get. If you don't feel the trust, do not give it.

Ralph Waldo Emerson said, *"Nothing is at last sacred but the integrity of your own mind."*

Of course, this does not mean you should be suspicious of everyone and never trust anyone. This practice would be hurtful to others and injure your relationships as well. After all, people want to be trusted and want to feel you trust them. When you feel comfortable, show your trust to others.

One of the best ways to receive more trust from others is to give trust to others by acting truthfully and honestly. To have a friend, you must first be a friend. Act on what you think and feel rather than what you think others want to see or hear. When others sense your high level of integrity, honesty and sincerity, you will have established a trust eliminating the need for people to protect themselves from you. You will also give yourself a reason to have more faith in your own security regarding them. Of course, if there is ever a perceived lack of honesty or integrity in a situation, this will provide a reason for skepticism or mistrust.

Before you can have any hope that anything you read in this book is going to help improve your life, you must first become your own person and trust your own judgment. Even if you currently have doubts about your own judgment, you simply must get closer in touch with your own feelings. It is not too hard. Gradually, you will withdraw from having such doubts and it will bring you to the place where you know it is only you making the decisions for you. At times, the number of different things on your mind will cause you to feel unsure or confused. However, you must remember it is not your mind but rather your feelings which will indicate whether your instincts are correct. When in doubt, connect with your feelings and wait for a clear signal, as it will always be there.

Trust is also found in life principles and laws we connect with every day. One example is the law of gravity. You can always trust it. Life principles and laws are God's or Nature's fundamentals that hold true in all situations. They are often defined as basic facts or laws of nature underlying how things work. These are the things we can instinctively trust without the need to have a special feeling in order to trust.

Life principles exist to help guide all living things. This is because there must be trust (a positive truth) we can all depend upon in order to give us the confidence to move forward. Because life principles don't change, they are dependable and therefore trustworthy.

We instinctively know many of life's natural principles like:

The motivation of people is guided by the basic need to preserve life.

The world runs on individuals pursuing their own self-interests (although that self interest may include being kind to others).

All people demand for themselves justice, fairness, and equality.

(People believe: "If they can do it, so can I")

All people know to threaten someone else is also to threaten themselves.

You can always rely on the principles and laws of physics such as the rotation of the sun, the tilt of the earth, and the shift of the tides.

However, you should mistrust anything violating nature's laws or life principles you instinctively know to be true. If someone offers you something that sounds like it is too good to be true then it probably is. The world commonly refers to this type of knowing as common sense.

Remember, the best way for you to ensure your safety is to trust yourself.

Like anyone, you will experience some trial and error and make a mistake now and then. However, you must continue to believe in your ability to trust yourself because you are the person who has the most interest in you. Furthermore, you are the person who will reap the benefits or consequences of your judgment.

Always trusting yourself is an absolute necessity to achieving greater happiness for yourself and your loved ones. Over time, you will not be disappointed.

SO, What Is The Wisdom In This Chapter and ...What Do You Do With This Information?

Self-defeating behaviors often develop as a response to a lack of trust in other alternatives available.

Understand the importance of trust in all your decision making regarding whether to move forward, remain still or step back.

Be your own person by trusting only you to take care of you.

The ability for you to know when to trust was given to you at birth by God or Mother Nature and it is revealed to you in the form of feelings. It is your choice to either ignore your feelings or to let them guide you, but the decision is always yours.

Regardless of whether you make a decision yourself or give your trust to another, remember it will always remain your responsibility.

Don't worry about your own lack of faith in your decision-making ability because this improves with trial and error over time.

Allow yourself to make some mistakes because that is the way you continue to learn.

Be trustworthy when dealing with others and you can expect to receive more trust from others in return. Trust is a precious gift and never given easily. Once trust is lost it is almost impossible to get back.

Use your own good common sense and never forget the best way for you to ensure your safety is to trust yourself.

CHAPTER 6

Your
"Guidance System"

What is it that alerts you when to sit down and when to get back up?

What is it that alerts you to step forward, step back or remain still?

What is it that helps you decide who to trust?

What is it that draws you toward one thing but away from another?

What is it that makes you do something others may not do?

In other words:

What is it that guides you in all things in your life?

Do you think you are guided by a part of your body like your liver? your kidneys? your lungs? or is it your parents? your teachers? your friends? or is it your religious faith? your destiny? or is it something else? While many things can influence you, what is the primary thing that guides you in your life?

Think of yourself like a ship steering on a course toward somewhere and with all the possible directions in front of you, you need some way to know what course to take. How would you know?

Fortunately, both you and all other human beings were born with an internal *guidance system* that navigates you through life. Everyone has their own guidance system working exclusively for them.

Your personal guidance system is made up of two primary things that guide you throughout your life:

They are:

Your Emotions and Intelligence

Or

Your Feelings and Thinking[1]

You become aware of your feelings from cues transmitted from inside your body and your senses such as your sight, hearing, touch, taste and smell.

In terms of your body, many would sum up your guidance system as your heart and your mind. God or Nature gave you

---

1   *This idea has been well documented in the Science of Deliberate Creation, the works of ABRAHAM, as told by Jerry and Ester Hicks, Abraham-Hicks Publications, L.L.C., 1989, www.abraham-hicks.com*

both of these at birth. They are already within you and you are free to use them as you deem fit. They do not control you but are simply there to guide you.

Ralph Waldo Emerson said, *"What lies behind us and what lies before us are small matters compared to what lies within us. And when we bring what is within us out into the world, miracles happen."*

While there are some parts of life that are not free for you to choose such as your need for oxygen and food, most everything else is guided by using your feelings and your intelligence in cooperation with one another.

It may be a unique idea for you to look at yourself as having a pre-installed guidance system before birth, but becoming aware of this now helps you understand how to guide yourself in future decision making.

When you think about it, without some sort of individual guidance system, you would have no way to know how to make decisions and therefore would inadvertently destroy yourself within a short period of time. If you were unable to make choices, you would not have free will. Therefore, you would be controlled.

The wisdom of the universe (defined here as God or Mother Nature) has been pre-installed within you and contains everything you need to successfully evolve on this earth.

It is appropriate here to note the difference between knowledge and wisdom. At birth, you were given wisdom. You acquired knowledge as you experienced life. Knowledge is a learned awareness and understanding of a person or thing whereas wisdom is the gift of knowing how to apply knowledge.

So, what is it that alerts you when to sit down and when to get up? The answer is your *feelings* for rest or comfort alert you to sit down and your *thought* of something you want to do alert you to get up.

What is it that causes you to step forward, step back or remain still? The answer is that when you *feel and think* you are safe, you will then step forward. If you do not feel this way, you will step back or remain still.

Your inner feelings are the part of your guidance system that provides the *absolute truth* about everything pertaining to you. Your feelings are the one thing you can always trust because they never lie to you. Their purpose is to guide you toward the truth (for you) so you don't go astray. Be aware and trust your feelings.

Differences

Since everyone's feelings are individual to them like fingerprints, you can only trust the feelings that come from you and no one else. Again, the best way for you to ensure your safety is to trust yourself.

Everyone in this world has a feeling about those things in which they come into contact, but not everyone feels exactly the same thing. For example, if you and I see a new car for the first time, I may love the design of the car and you may hate it. But how did we know what we liked and didn't like without ever experiencing it before? It is the inner wisdom within each individual. Your body will always tell you what is in harmony with you and what is not by giving you either a positive or a negative feeling towards someone or something.

Picture two girlfriends walking down the street next to one another and a young man is walking towards both of them. Suddenly one girlfriend says to the other, "that is one good looking guy!" The other girlfriend immediately says, "you think so, I think he's a dog." Well, what's the truth? Is he a good-looking guy or not?

The answer is that he is good looking to one girl but not the other. This often occurs because people have a unique and innate sense of what is in sync or harmony with them. This is their guiding light. Our guidance system is there to push us to evolve toward a better place within the universe. It is God's or Nature's way of providing alternatives to help the earth continually choose, evolve and prosper.

Please recognize both girls never saw this guy before but they both had a definite feeling and opinion about him. How is this possible? Where did this feeling come from? How is it that I like the color blue but not orange? If you see a tree, a car, a building, or a person, you have an immediate reaction to it. Our senses are part of our guidance system and allow us to like or dislike different smells, tastes, and sounds. These things help us to realize something is guiding us, not controlling us, from within.

Therefore, the lesson is to always listen to your body.

Two Equal Parts

With that said, it is interesting to note that your feelings do not offer you an explanation regarding why they are giving you a positive or negative signal. But it is the second part of your guidance system, your thinking or intelligence, which has the ability to give you a logical explanation of why you received the feeling.

When both your feelings and thinking are in agreement, you are good to go because your guidance system is in alignment. When your thinking is not in agreement with a feeling, you will immediately receive a negative feeling, alerting you to stop until both parts of your guidance system (emotional and rational) are aligned.

For example, people with hurt emotional feelings cannot always resolve their emotional pain through thinking because they don't give their rational thinking equal weight to balance their feelings. They often say they understand why it is logical and rational that they should not feel so badly but they can't help feeling that way.

If this is true for you, answer this question: If your intelligence tells you that something is illogical or irrational and doesn't make sense to you, how do you allow yourself to dismiss or disregard this part of your guidance system? Your guidance system consists of TWO PARTS to help you balance your life. It is not okay to ignore any part of your guidance system which was given to you to help you make the right decisions for you. How do you justify to yourself proceeding with something that is illogical and irrational? If you do, you will always be wrong and continue to live an illusion. I know it is hard to release the emotional hurt you have felt for years just because it doesn't make sense intellectually … BUT

YOU MUST USE YOUR INTELLECT TOO. Remember that you are almost always more aware of your feelings than your thinking because thinking usually requires more concentration and effort whereas feelings do not. It is also understandable that you might feel stupid or resentful that you held onto your hurt feelings all these years when it was so easy to release the hurt by simply giving your intelligence and emotions equal weight.

SO, What Is The Wisdom In This Chapter and ...What Do You Do With This Information?

The wisdom here is to recognize you have a magnificent guidance system within you to use to more effectively enrich your life. It is another precious gift, pre-installed at birth, that allows you to access the wisdom of your world so you can evolve to whatever you aspire to be.

Listen to your body at all times, using the positive feelings and thoughts you receive to step forward. Your guidance system is perfect because it contains all the wisdom (not knowledge) you need to accomplish any human purpose. You have to listen to your body more diligently and access the wisdom within by being aware of your feelings and thoughts and act when they are both in agreement.

You do not have to go outside yourself to find the answers you seek in life. You may have to go outside of yourself for added knowledge about things in life, but you have the ability within to make the final decision by listening to your guidance system.

CHAPTER 7

Respect The Things Around You

[Don't Fear Them—Don't Try To Control
Them—Keep Things Balanced]

elf-defeating behaviors develop when people are afraid to
act honestly because they anticipate an unfavorable reaction
or believe they cannot control the outcome of events, when
all they really need to do is be in harmony with all things or
recognize that there are always other alternatives.

To keep yourself grounded in all things, it is important
that you don't fear things around you or try to control them
either. All things within which you come into contact during

your life have different qualities you need to be aware of and respect to find harmony in your world.

The concept of respect really means "acceptance of what is". You do not necessarily need to agree with it or admire it, but you have to at least accept that it exists and not disrespect it.

An example of this respect is a quote by the famous French author and philosopher Voltaire who is believed to have said:

"I disapprove of what you say, but I will defend to the death your right to say it".

The term harmony is the concept of "being in sync or in balance" so each party derives comparable benefit from the other and neither party considers the relationship or arrangement to be unfair or unbalanced.

When you are aware of and respect the different qualities of others, there is no reason to fear them or try to control them to make your life safe. This chapter will help you to minimize the influence of fear in your life as a basis for your actions. It will also help to reduce or eliminate your desire or your perceived need to control things. Rather it will encourage you to keep all things balanced.

Fear

Ralph Waldo Emerson said, *"Fear defeats more people than any other one thing in the world."*

Too many people act out of fear.

Michael Jordon, the basketball star, said that, *"Fear is an illusion."* Therefore, the logic goes, don't allow an illusion or faulty perception to consume, influence or rule your actions.

President Franklin D. Roosevelt said, *"The only thing we have to fear is fear itself."*

People typically fear things they do not understand and then create an illusion they are in danger, become fearful and overly defensive. If they simply tried to understand the situation and recognized there is nothing trying to harm them or that they have the capability of avoiding any possible harmful effects, there would be no reason for fear in the first place.

Unfortunately, people's lives are filled with fear because they don't choose to evaluate and then respect things not immediately known to them and therefore imagine potential harm simply as a precaution.

If you think about it, there is nothing in this world intentionally trying to hurt you. There are objects and people that can hurt you, just like you could hurt others. Two important things stopping people from hurting others is a lack of desire to see anyone hurt or because they don't want to risk getting hurt themselves.

If you unreasonably fear people or objects that would not hurt you, your fear is an illusion and your subsequent actions may be inappropriate and possibly harmful because they are based on an illusion. For example, if you fear a homeless man who has not threatened you in any way and you try to scare him away, he might then feel threatened and become aggressive.

Ask yourself, do you fear a snowflake? Of course not would be your reply. Do your fear a bunch of snowflakes packed 12 inches high on the road when you are driving? Some people would say "yes" even though the snowflake has no intention of hurting you and doesn't even know you exist.

So why would you fear it?

Realistically, when you think about it there is no reason for you to be afraid. However, there is a reason for you to be aware and respect the truth in this situation. The truth here is that when a bunch of snowflakes come together on a road, the road then becomes slippery. If you are not aware and respectful of this fact and drive normally, you could get into an accident and be injured. Like most things, there is no reason to fear the snow if you respect its properties and then drive cautiously. This includes watching the other drivers too. Remember, the snowflake doesn't even know that you exist so it couldn't be trying to hurt you.

Fear comes from uncertainty and causes anxiety leading you to overreact to the situation and put yourself in unnecessary danger. Putting yourself in unnecessary danger is unsafe. Being aware of the truth about snow and respecting its properties removes your anxiety and danger because you are motivated to simultaneously slow down and proceed with caution and safety in the snow, as in life.

Consider another example. Suppose you see a car coming toward you at 60 mph. If you don't get out of its path you believe it will kill you. Should you be afraid of that car? My answer is "no" because the car is not intending to hurt you and doesn't even know you are in its path. However, you must be aware and respect the truth that if you don't get out of the way of this 4,000 lb. vehicle then it will kill you. You don't have to fear the car, you only need to respect its power and get out of its way. Let us say that ten seconds later that same car comes to a stop near you. Should you be afraid to go over and touch that car now? Of course not! The truth is the car is an inanimate object, cannot have any intensions of hurting you, and doesn't even know you exist. You must respect the power of a car, but there is no reason to fear it. There is a big difference between having fear and having respect.

Do you think people should fear you because you can hurt them if you choose? The answer is "no." However, what they should be aware of and respect is that if they try to hurt you, they may need to fear your response. Fear comes from an uncertainty about the future whereas being aware and respecting the circumstances of the situation and the people involved eliminates a need for fear and anxiety so you can move forward with a reasonable degree of trust and safety.

Learn to be aware and respectful of your surroundings and your can eliminate fear in your life. Your decisions will yield a better result.

Nelson Mandela said, *"I learned that courage was not the absence of fear, but the triumph over it. The brave man is not he who does not feel afraid, but the one who conquers that fear."*

Regardless of how logical my words might sound, they may not be easy for you to accept because of your past thinking and experiences. If I always challenge fear, I will never be ruled by it. Rather than being fearful of life, I prefer to live life. You may have emotionally developed a habit of fearing things you don't know or are not sure of. With that said, let's go one-step further in order to try and help you remove most fear and anxiety as a part of your future feelings.

It might be helpful for me to explain why I am less fearful of things other people do fear:

Fear of a barking dog that is approaching me.

If the dog's tail is wagging, I can rest assured he is not intending to cause harm. If it's not wagging, I stay still so he can sniff me. I respect his need to feel safe and to protect his loved ones. If I did not act aggressively, he should have no reason to attack me and I should not have a reason to fear him. If he does get aggressive, which I don't expect, I will first try to move away or, if necessary, kick him so he will begin to feel my response to his aggression. I have choices.

Fear of a drunk walking toward me in the street.

If he approaches me, I will appear disinterested or preoccupied or simply tell him to move on. I will never appear fearful because I don't want him to feel I will easily back down if he chooses to bother me. If he does start to annoy me, I will move away, call for assistance or confront him.

Fear that I will fail a test at school.

If I studied, I have little to fear. However, if I didn't study, I must accept the result. My next step is to prepare for the *consequences*, learn from my mistake, and study harder for my next test.

Fear that a sniper or crazy man will kill me or an airplane will crash when I'm aboard.

These scenarios are far too unlikely to even worry about because of the odds. In these types of situations, I choose to worry less about protecting my life and more about enjoying it. I believe my natural instincts and common sense will protect me.

<u>Fear about going on a job interview.</u>

Having self-worth and training in your field will not guarantee you will get a job. If you appear anxious, needy, or fearful of not getting a job, your interviewer will see your desperation and lack of confidence, hesitating to give you the job. Go with what you have and present it in the most truthful and favorable manner. There is no need to fear the interview as you will ultimately get a job.

<u>Fear about being able to make enough money.</u>

Money is a natural consequence of what you do and the value your services have to others. Prepare yourself to be in a position of value and the money will come. There is nothing to fear because you are in-charge and no one is stopping you.

<u>Fear that my wife may leave me.</u>

It would never happen. I'm too cute.

While most things may work out the way you imagine, some situations will not. Because there are numerous variables in life, it is impossible to guarantee anything. Please don't expect guarantees. Even if I promise to be at a certain place at a certain time, that promise is always contingent on specific unknowns. There are always many unforeseen obstacles that could arise, preventing my arrival at any particular destination.

Please begin to accept life disappointments with the same level of maturity in which you accept life accomplishments. While disappointments are only temporary, they offer the opportunity to learn. Every disappointment opens up novel opportunities for new accomplishments. Every problem is simply an opportunity in disguise.

You can always encourage yourself to look for the opportunities and reach for them without guarantees or fear of failure.

With all of these considerations in mind, there are experiences in life you should fear.

The greatest fear in life you can experience is holding onto false beliefs that are not real truths. There is a real truth always present and existing in our world whether you choose to believe it or not. This truth is based on steadfast worldly and universal principles created by the laws of physics, God and nature, all of which affect everything in your life. If you choose to believe something that is not the real truth, then the real truth will not go away but rather continue to influence the outcome of your actions in life.

Your lack of willingness to see the real truth in life is the one scenario to fear.

Control

Too many people try to manipulate or control the people in their life in the hope of getting what they want or avoiding what they don't want.

Michael Jordon also said, *"Control is an illusion."*

The idea you can control a person or any living being is an illusion because the concept is in direct opposition to the natural order of the universe. The idea of control is an idea that will inhibit free will, growth and development, which will stunt the evolution of life.

This fact was emphasized in the movie *Jurassic Park*. In this movie, Dr. Hammond, the developer of Jurassic Park, tried to clone and control the sex of the dinosaurs by creating only females. Dr. Malcolm, a Keynesian scientist played by Jeff Goldbloom, told Dr. Hammond, "this type of control is not possible. The history of evolution has taught us that "Life will not be contained. Life breaks through." This concept further applies to our unrealistic attempts to control others. Any attempt at control will cause a rebellion to break out, as ultimately happened with the animals in Jurassic Park.

"You can't fool with Mother Nature."

So, instead of trying to control living things in your life, learn how to be in harmony with all living things because no one will accept being controlled. It is imperative to give up control as a way to get what you want. Rather than pushing people to do things they don't want to do, clearly explain or demonstrate to them why they should do those same things and how they will find benefit in them. Through this behavior, you will alleviate unnecessary resistance and create a positive experience and environment for everyone. Since the truth will benefit them or things they care about, you can reduce your future risk of being discovered as a liar or lose the trust of others and the relationships they offer.

If you think about it, God and Mother Nature do not attempt to control us. They created brilliant universal laws and principles that sustain the earth. By giving us at birth both internal wisdom and free will, we have the ability to use these laws and principles as we see fit to help us and our world continue to evolve.

(Don't lose sight of the fact that all this is connected to self-defeating behaviors.)

The Law of Balance

When travelling through your life, an important universal principle to understand is the Law of Balance.

Self-defeating behaviors develop when your life is out of balance.

Euripides, the Greek philosopher, said, *"The best and safest thing is to keep balance in your life, acknowledge the great powers around us and in us. If you can do that, and live that way, you are really a wise man."*

Everything in the world seeks balance and you must do the same in your life. Keeping balance in your life is a little known innate drive, but is also essential to happiness because those things out of balance are unsettling. That is why even the simplest of things off balance can cause discomfort such as the need to straighten a tilted picture on the wall.

The most important tool in building any structure is not a saw or a hammer but rather a Level. Why? … because it insures balance. Anything that is not balanced is by definition out of balance and is at risk to fall. Balance is a powerful force created in our world to maintain strength, stability and ensure all options are considered before actions take place. The Greek philosophers expressed it as *"moderation in all things."* This means too much or too little of one thing is usually a bad thing –balance is best.

Tyrants, disease, greed, dishonesty or some other negative force would overtake the earth if it didn't maintain its balance through the millions of years of existence. There was always something that came along as a counterbalance.

For example, if it weren't for balance, the trillions of insects on earth could control the world. The balance in this scenario is that, while the insects have a purpose, the birds and other creatures eat the insects and maintain a healthy balance. There have been and continue to be species of animals and plants that went extinct and replaced by new species, all for the purpose of evolving to maintain a balance for our world.

Sir Isaac Newton best expressed the law of balance when he wrote: *"For every action there is an equal and opposite reaction."*

You probably remember this principle from school but may not have ever fully understood its powerful impact on your life.

Self-defeating behaviors arise when things are unbalanced such as a one-sided relationship.

A simple example of balance is seen in the statement: You can never take three steps toward something without also taking exactly three steps away from something else. Whether you recognize it or not, everything you do causes something opposite to happen with the same strength or value. This is enormously valuable for you to realize whenever you need to make decisions in your life. Knowing with certainty that your every action will cause an opposite reaction helps you to more carefully consider your choices.

The balance that exists is frequently expressed in many ways in our daily life. Here are some examples to help solidify the idea within you:

- "Do unto others as you would have others do unto you."
- "As ye sow, so shall ye reap."
- "The greater the risk, the greater the reward."
- "The deeper the love, the greater the loss."
- "The taller the tree, the bigger the root."
- "The deeper the hole, the harder it is to crawl out." (How hard is it to crawl out? Exactly in proportion to the depth of the hole.)
- "The pain of death creates an equal appreciation of life."
- "The closer you move toward something, the further you move away from something else."
- "The only way to have a friend is to be a friend."
- "You cannot help someone else without helping yourself at the same time."
- "The avoidance of one thing attracts another thing."
- "The more something is controlled, the less freedom it has."
- "The more restrictions, the less chance for change."
- "If you don't give people the benefit of the doubt, you take away their chance to succeed."
- "People who have little money worry about getting it and people who have a lot of money worry about losing it."
- "With great power comes great responsibility."
- "Every problem is also an opportunity."

There are thousands of such examples and they all demonstrate the balance in life. By now, you should see how important the principle of balance is to your life.

Again, self-defeating behaviors develop when things in your life are out of balance.

The law of balance is part of the great wisdom of the universe and is designed to be the great equalizer of all things. It seeks to maintain opposites so any one thing cannot gain total control over another. It seeks to maintain opposites so that each thing can be valued when compared to its counterpart. It seeks to maintain opposites so that each thing can be evaluated in terms of its contributions to survival of the world in order to continue to evolve to a better place.

We all encounter bad things throughout our life. When these things happen, we tend to see the bad or feel the hurt without recognizing what good also came with the bad. It would be very beneficial if you could learn to look for the good and bad in everything. For example:

- Knowing that death is inevitable is what gives you an appreciation for life and is also the great equalizer of all things.
- Losing your job gives you the incentive and opportunity to find a better job.
- Making a mistake teaches you how to avoid similar mistakes in the future.

- You can tell your child "hot, hot, hot" one hundred times but it is not until he burns his little finger for the first time that he is protected for life.
- While the rain may slow business on the beach it causes sales of umbrellas to soar.
- The death of the father can make the boy become a man.

Positive and negative are inseparable. Look for both in all things.

Balance exists everywhere but not always at the same moment in time. Some life examples: A person you hurt in some way may not choose to retaliate against you until sometime later; or the effects of excess sugar you eat may not reveal itself until you are later diagnosed with diabetes; or a good deed by you may not be repaid until sometime later when the other person has the opportunity to do so.

Another life example would be if your car won't start one morning and you ask your neighbor to drive you to work, which is a favor which your neighbor would subconsciously expect you to return if he or she was ever in the same situation. Why? In the interest of fairness (balance).

Your neighbor may not require any repayment but because you allowed your neighbor to do you a good turn, you also created the (unknowing) expectation by your neighbor that you would do the same for him or her if the occasion arose. In a way, by accepting the help of your neighbor, you have created an unspoken debt which you must realistically acknowledge that you owe to your neighbor. If you do not recognize you're debt when and if the occasion arises, your neighbor will consider you unfair, inconsiderate and unappreciative and may refuse to help you again. This is all part of the Law of Balance.

People Who Seek Perfection Are Really Seeking Balance

You may consider yourself a perfectionist.

Perfection refers to something flawless or faultless in its design or ability to accomplish its purpose. A perfectionist is someone who pursues perfection.

When it comes to inanimate objects such as a watch, a calculator, a machine tool, etc., perfection is possible. However, when it comes to relationships between two living things with free will, the pursuit of perfection means the pursuit of balance. In fact, the degree of balance defines the degree of perfection because there is no opposition.

For example, the reason a show horse and his rider will win first prize is because of the balance achieved between the horse and the rider. The horse or the rider cannot win alone. They rely upon one another and need to be in harmony to achieve the desired outcome.

Remember when something is not in-balance, then by definition it is out-of-balance. Things that are out of balance are more vulnerable to collapse. Seek to maintain balance in all things in your life.

SO, What Is The Wisdom In This Chapter and ...What Do You Do With This Information?

Fear is an illusion. Stop being afraid. Use your common sense. Don't fear things that are not deliberately trying to hurt you. However, don't allow yourself to be hurt accidentally either. Understand the properties of all things and respect them. This is especially true involving your relationships with people.

Control is an illusion. Don't try to control things that would not want to be controlled for the mere purpose of receiving some temporary benefit. Instead, be in harmony with all things and people so the outcome is a win-win situation for all, without the risk of a future backlash.

Perfection is Balance. Remember to keep your life balanced by not trying to gain unfair advantages for yourself at the expense of others. Rather, do for yourself without being unfair to others. At the same time, don't do for others at the expense of yourself. Everyone, including you, deserves fairness. Remember that when anything is not in balance it is, by definition, out-of-balance and vulnerable to collapse.

(Don't lose sight of the fact that all this is connected to self-defeating behaviors.)

CHAPTER 8

Depression:
A Result of Anger

Self-defeating behaviors are frequent in people who are depressed.

At some point in our lives, we all experienced the feeling of being down or depressed. If this feeling persists, it can become a serious debilitating condition. Depression affects how you feel, think and behave. Depression can lead to a variety of emotional and physical problems.

Depression is so prevalent that about one third of shoplifters are believed to be suffering from depression on some level. However, few people know the real clinical definition of depression and how they can resolve it within themselves. The definition of depression provides the clue to resolving it.

Definition: *Depression is anger turned inward toward yourself.*

The opposite is aggression, which is anger turned outward toward others.

If you are depressed (in the absence of any chemical imbalance), you are most probably holding onto anger within. This anger is unconsciously directed towards you because of all the things you did or didn't do over the years that created the unhappy state you find yourself in today. It often means you didn't speak up for yourself or stand up for what you believe in when you should have. Although you may not feel or act like an angry person, this is likely because you may have repressed or hidden your inner feelings from yourself and others.

Penelope Sweet, famous author, wrote: *"Depression is nourished by a lifetime of ungrieved and unforgiven hurts."*

Although your anger may originate from the actions of others, it is inevitably turned inward toward yourself because you were unable to resolve it. Had you settled your anger at the time of the initial incident or closely thereafter, it would unlikely lead to depression.

However, because you did not resolve your issue(s), they remained inside you because it was the only way you knew how to handle them at the time.

People who experience depression are people who unconsciously blame themselves for allowing past issues to go unresolved. Part of recovery from depression is forgiving yourself and accepting the choices you made were the best choices you could think of at the time.

To understand depression a little deeper, anger develops and remains in your system through a cycle that involves hurt, blame and then anger. When you feel hurt by someone or something and your hurt feelings are not resolved to your satisfaction, you naturally begin to blame that someone or something for hurting you.

For example, if John doesn't apologize or take back a hurtful comment, you may get angry or "pissed" at John. Because John was the one who hurt you, you believe he is the only one who can correct the situation or fix the hurt you feel. This may be logical but is not correct thinking.

If you leave it to John to fix your hurt, what you are really doing is giving John your power which you could use to fix the hurt yourself. If John then doesn't fix it with an apology or in some other manner to make amends, you conclude that you have no choice but to remain angry.

A crucial thing to remember is never give away your power to resolve your hurt to another person by believing that it is the other person's responsibility. Whether the hurt occurred today or thirty years ago, you can fix it without the help or need of the person who initiated this pain. The majority of depression is the result of holding onto unresolved issues from the past. Even though the people and circumstances that caused your anger may no longer exist, you still have the power to resolve your anger from the past.

The way to avoid holding onto anger is for you to remove the blame from the hurt, blame, anger equation.

Dr. Albert Ellis, eminent psychologist, said:

"You largely constructed your depression. It wasn't given to you. Therefore, you can deconstruct it."

To resolve your issues, first realize there are many possible reasons why a person might have done or said something which hurt you. If what they said or did was not truthful, then they had the problem, not you. However, if what they said or did was truthful, then you should apologize or make amends for whatever was done and you can then hopefully move on without anger.

There are a number of reasons why persons might hurt you. They could be jealous of you; could have believed something they heard about you which was untrue; had a fight with a loved one that morning and wanted to lash out at someone; wanted you to share their values and be like them; been under the influence of medication or you may have unknowingly 'pushed their button' and upset them. It really doesn't make a lot of difference what their problem is. In fact, there is a good chance you may never figure it out. So what! Just realize that what you felt was not because of something you did but rather, because of something within the other person. It is their problem and you need to truly recognize that. Even though you were affected by what they said or did, you cannot take it personally because if you were not there, the hurt would probably have been directed toward someone else.

Don't keep suffering from depression or anger because of something that was never your fault or your problem in the first place. You must be willing to see the truth.

Because we all experience hurt, blame and anger situations going back to childhood, if the anger experienced is not released and resolved, it can then be stored inside us and cause us to either become an angry person or appear as a calm person and express anger in a different manner. The evidence of unresolved anger is often hidden in withdrawal or rage.

Many times, the anger inside us is so deep and repressed it is not even experienced as anger.

You may say, "I'm not an angry person." However, if you experience depression, there is a high probability you have repressed anger that is negatively affecting your daily life. In the absence of any other logical explanation, it might be wise for you to consider the reason you might be depressed is because you are angry inside. With that said, you still have to settle within yourself what someone said or did. One way to do this is to understand what happened and accept it was not intended to be malicious. Another way is to realize the person who hurt you is not as good a friend as you had thought or was a little "off" in his or her thinking. As a result, you may choose to distance yourself from that person or decide to no longer have contact with him or her. Whatever the case may be, the final decision is yours.

A person who develops depression can resolve the emotional issues from the past on their own through releasing blame. Without blame, there cannot be any anger. You do not have to forgive the people who hurt you in the past, but you should consider the real truth about the past and find a good reason to release the blame and anger that follows.

In your search for the real truth, also consider whether you should take any (or all) responsibility for your action(s) contributing to your hurt.

I previously told you how I released the blame I felt about my birth mother leaving me, my adopted mother for not loving me, my adopted parents for getting divorced and later my birth mother for rejecting me as her son. While these things hurt me, it is clear none of the decisions made by others were intentionally designed to hurt me. Everyone had their own personal reasons which had nothing to do with me.

If you still have unresolved issues with your childhood, parents or family, it is not only because of your past experiences, but also because of your own unwillingness to release the blame you attribute to yourself or others.

SO, What Is The Wisdom In This Chapter and ... What Do You Do With This Information?

Self-defeating behaviors frequently develop in people who are depressed.

Depression is most frequently a state of mind.

The definition of depression is anger turned inward toward yourself. You are angry at yourself because of the things you did or did not do to resolve the hurt you still feel.

Depression is created by our own mind as a way to cope with hurt we believe we cannot resolve in any other way. We feel helpless but the truth is that we can resolve the hurt caused by others from within ourselves. This means most depression is not a condition we need to live with or face in the future.

Depression is the result of our inability to recognize the real truth in a situation and to quickly resolve the issue with either an apology or our realization that it is the other person that has a personal problem.

Knowing that the world runs on individuals pursuing their own self-interests, it is a fair assumption that the person who hurt you was seeking something for themselves rather than intending to hurt you. Therefore, consider their possible motivations and look for what makes the most sense to you.

Understand how hurt and blame can then develop into anger and, if left unresolved, develop into a state of depression. You only need to release the blame which allowed the anger to develop in the first place. And, when you see the truth about what caused your hurt, your blame, anger and depression will be gone.

Resolving you're hurt is not another person's responsibility, it is your responsibility.

The next chapter will help you to understand exactly how to release your hurt, blame and anger without the unwelcomed and unnecessary discomfort that sometimes comes with it.

(Don't lose sight of the fact that all this is connected to self-defeating behaviors.)

CHAPTER 9

Replace False Beliefs
With The Real Truth

Think about how many times you have heard the phrase, *"The truth will set you free."*

Mahatma Gandhi said, *"There is no God higher than the truth."*

In a world filled with unknowns, the truth is the only thing you can count on in your life. It is consistently reliable and therefore trustworthy.

Truth exists about all things and the outcome of all things is ultimately shaped by the truth.

Terry Leahy, former Tesco CEO said: *"The truth is the best compass to guide on through the storms."*

Self-defeating behaviors are almost always the result of false beliefs you hold and a lack of awareness of the truth or a lack of confidence to explore alternatives available.

Remember that just because you choose to believe something doesn't make it the truth. The real truth always remains just that, whether you choose to believe it or not. An excellent example of this is that you were born as a perfect human being and this will always be true whether you choose to believe it or not.

We have all heard the phrase 'Truth is in the eye of the beholder.' What this means is that if a person perceives something is true, then it becomes the truth to them and they will act on it. However, this kind of truth is a perceived truth, and may not be the real truth pertaining to a particular situation. Different people can have different ideas about what is the truth in the exact same situation. However, I must tell you that if the belief you hold is negative about you as a person, it is almost guaranteed to be false and you should not allow yourself to readily accept it. For example, I may think I will never amount to anything worthwhile because my father drilled it into my head but others may see me as a person with great potential.

It is important for you to search for the real truth in all situations as best you can so you aren't making life choices based on false beliefs. Let's find the truth to the following question and help you to see how the real truth can then set you free.

Is the Glass Half-Full or Half-Empty?

Psychologists often use the analogy of a half-full / half-empty glass to evaluate whether a person's outlook is optimistic or pessimistic and positive or negative. This question asks for a person's perception of the truth, which may or may not be the real one. In the context of your life, it is more valuable for you to know the real truth rather than maintaining your current perception of it.

If given a glass half filled with water, from your perspective, what is the answer to the question?

Is the glass half-full or half-empty?

You might say your answer would depend on which day you were asked the question and whether you were in a positive or negative mood. However, the truth I am looking for does not depend upon your feeling on any given day. I am looking for you to learn the truth on every day.

If you said the glass is half-full, that is the incorrect answer.

If you said the glass is half-empty that is also the incorrect answer.

The correct answer to the question is that the glass is neither half-full nor half-empty but rather the glass is completely full. This is not a trick answer but is rather the real truth. While half the glass is filled with water, the other half is filled with air. I do not mean to be funny. Air should not be viewed as nothing because it lifts giant aircraft into the sky. In this scenario, "completely full" is the absolute truth. To demonstrate this point to yourself, please answer these questions:

Is there any way to add water to the glass without removing the air? Is there any way to add air to the glass without removing the water?

Your answer must be "no" to both of these questions.

While perception may not always be truth, another lesson learned from this experiment is that in our world, *you can never put something into something else without first taking something out.*

This applies to almost everything you do including your thinking and feelings. When you remove a false belief and replace it with the truth, the false belief is gone and truth will then set you free.

It is important for you to know and remember every space in our world is filled with something - whether it is air, water, dust, a thought or a feeling. There is no vacuum on our earth. Therefore, it is a universal law that before you can change your mind or feeling about something, you must remove and replace a previous feeling or thought already there.

This is called the Law of Displacement and is the mechanism we all should use to effect personal change. You may have more free space in your brain to store information, but your brain cannot hold two opposing thoughts in the space you already used. If you try to add an opposing thought or a contradictory feeling within your body, then you would complicate things because your brain could not determine from which space to find an answer. Thus, one thought, one feeling, one spot is imperative to your brain and its ability to focus and work correctly.

Since you can't live in two places at once such as the past and the present, you have to choose and, as always, the choice is yours.

Although people talk about changing their mind or currently feeling a certain way about something, you really cannot change your mind or feelings. Rather, you must remove the old in order to make room for the new. By doing this, your body will have one specific thought or feeling about an issue on which to base its future actions. Removal of your old truth (false belief) and replacement with your new belief (the real truth) will help set you free regarding any issue you face.

Consider the following examples of how false beliefs can be replaced with real truths:

False Beliefs	*Real Truths*
1. "My father loved my brother more than me because he picked on me so much more."	The *real truth* may be that because you were older and more capable than your brother, his expectations of you were greater even though he never told you how he felt. Or, the *real truth* may also be that your father was a real SOB and his treatment of you was the result of his own insecurity or inner anger toward others directed at someone who couldn't or wouldn't fight back. It had nothing to do with you.

2.	"My mother didn't care enough about me because she never protected me from my abusive father."	The *real truth* may be that your mother was tormented by your father's treatment of you but was afraid that he would become worse if she interfered and possibly turn around and become abusive to her.
3.	"If it wasn't for a few people in my life, I would be OK."	The *real truth* is that it is rarely the actions of others which cause your problems in life but rather your response to others actions. You can always choose to flee, fight, understand or accept those faults in others.
4.	"What happened in the past can't be erased."	The *real truth* is that the past is gone forever and can only be in your present and future if you allow it to be there. You can remember the past *without* allowing it to torment you in the present and future.
5.	"I am too old and too fixed in my ways to change now."	The *real truth* is that you change your mind in many ways every day. You only seem fixed because you wish to hold onto false beliefs because you are fearful of having to deal with the real truth.

6. "I am too insecure to try new things."	The *real truth* is that, as was discussed in earlier chapters, learn to trust yourself and you will begin to feel and become more secure within you.
7. "I will never be able to forgive myself for what I have done."	Yes you will. The *real truth* is that doing a bad thing does not make you a bad person. You owe it to yourself to understand that you were under real emotional pain when you did whatever you did because your actions were out of character for you. It is unrealistic for you to be unwilling to forgive yourself for being human. Your feelings of guilt prove you deserve it.
8. "I am too fat & too ugly to be loved."	The *real truth* is that you are not too fat and too ugly in everyone's eyes. You just see yourself that way. You know you are a beautiful person inside but you falsely choose to believe that this doesn't count. In reality, it is the only thing that counts on a lasting basis.

9. "I feel guilty about everything."	The *real truth* is that anger inside you led you to frequently *overreact* to people or situations. It is your *overreaction* that has caused you to feel guilty. You can learn how to resolve the anger which led to your overreaction and the feelings of guilt that followed.
10. "I will never be good enough."	The *real truth* is that you were born good enough but others in your life didn't appreciate your worth and you allowed yourself to believe them.

Could any of these false beliefs apply to you? If not, do you have similar false beliefs that negatively impact your life?

These examples should demonstrate that whatever your circumstances are, there may be another way to look at it, which also may be closer to the truth. You can only benefit by opening up your mind and being willing to consider other possibilities, even though those scenarios may create hurt from the past. However, if you still hurt from your past, you have not seen the truth about your past. Although, if you honestly decide what you currently believe is the real truth, there is no reason to replace your current belief.

It is not hard to remove a false belief and replace it with a new belief once you see the truth. For example, if you felt angry at your friend because she made a false statement about you to others, you would probably blame her for defaming you and be angry. You would replace your former good feelings toward her with bad ones. However, if she subsequently told others what she said was false and meant as a joke, you would immediately release anger toward her and replace it with good feelings again. While you may admire other qualities in your friend, you could not feel both good and bad toward her about this issue at the same time.

SO, What Is The Wisdom In This Chapter and ... What Do You Do With This Information?

In order to make change within yourself and your life, you must first remove the false beliefs currently within and replace them with something else you believe is closer to the truth. When an old belief is replaced with a new belief, the old belief and your problem is gone forever.

Noted philosopher, psychologist & author William James said,

"It is our attitude at the beginning of a task which, more than anything else, will affect its successful outcome."

In other words, people can alter their lives by altering their attitude of mind. What this means is you can actually change your life without changing anything outside yourself simply by altering your attitude inside yourself? This is powerful!

The only permanent solution is to replace your current false beliefs about yourself or others with the real truth. You might ask, "What is the real truth?" It is the truth that consistently applies to all people under the exact same circumstances. The real truth is always revealed to us by the unwavering, steadfast principles that are clear whenever we affectionately connect with the wisdom within us. You will know the truth when you are willing to see it.

Remember that there is a difference between the real truth and one that is perceived.

The truth is often said to be in the eye of the beholder. This kind of truth is the perceived truth, and is often not the real truth. Different people develop different opinions about what is the truth in the same situation. The real truth about you is almost always positive and applies to most human beings because it is grounded to some universal principle in life which can never change.

Furthermore, there are basic truths that apply to all human beings that we all need to acknowledge in order to simplify the search for our own truth. For example, everyone needs to breath, eat and use the bathroom. We all need to feel secure about our ability to survive and also need to love and be loved.

Here are a dozen real truths that we can all recognize and depend upon:

- No one wants to make their life any harder than it is already.
- No one wants to be physically hurt.
- No one wants anyone to steal from them.
- No one wants to be misled.
- No one wants to be treated with disrespect.
- No one wants their life partner to be unfaithful.

- No one wants anyone to be disloyal or betray them.
- No one wants their freedom to be taken away.
- No one wants to be rejected by their peers.
- No one wants to feel unworthy.
- No one wants to be poor.
- No one wants to be ill.

These are only a few of life's truths as it pertains to all of us and we can rely on these types of truths when making decisions to go forward. This gives us a feeling of comfort and safety. It is my hope you have been able to absorb and begin to apply the wisdom contained in this book so that you can say with confidence: *"The dragon doesn't live here anymore."* [2]

---

2   *Taken from the title of a book by author Alan H. Cohen.*

CHAPTER 10

Ongoing Support and Psychotherapy

One of the best things you can do for yourself is ask for help when you are unsure how to go forward or feel you cannot do it alone. Getting help is a brave and sensible thing to do as it demonstrates both your commitment to change and your faith that you will find a personal resolution. Your willingness to seek the real truth rather than hold onto false beliefs is courageous. It may not be easy task to share your secrets and attempt to change your behavior in a positive manner. If you maintain this positive attitude through your journey, you will almost certainly accomplish your goals. It is just a matter of time. You have nothing to fear because whatever truth you discover will only help to set you free.

How To Ask

Before you can find comfort in revealing your secret and seeking help, you should feel secure your confidentiality will be protected and at ease with the person or agency you choose.

There are different kinds of support available to you.

You may begin by going to the website: www.PeterBerlinAuthor-AddictionCoach.com for a wide range of services. Click on the box which shows "Personal Coaching" or *"Other Resources"*.

You can always search www.Google.com for a larger list of resources.

In addition, here are three authors you may want to consider reading if you wish to go further into your self-improvement quest:

- Alan H. Cohen – "Why Your Life Sucks …"
- Jack Canfield – "Chicken Soup for the Soul"
- P. McGraw (Dr. Phil) – "Creating Your Life from the Inside Out"

Before you make a decision to proceed with psychotherapy here are some things you should know.

Psychotherapy

The decision to engage in psychotherapy is an important one because it provides a special opportunity to explore the basic beliefs behind your behaviors and helps you to find the real truth about you.

When Should You Consider Psychotherapy?

There are a number of scenarios regarding when you should consider psychotherapy including:

Traumatic Life Event

Consider psychotherapy if you have experienced a traumatic life event (recently or earlier in life) which you believe may be responsible for the onset or acceleration of your self-defeating behavior. Some examples of traumatic life events include: a divorce, the serious illness or loss of a loved one, your loss of health, loss of income, loss of savings or investments, or even a large increase in expenses.

A traumatic life event can threaten your basic needs and push you into a tailspin. This can then cause added difficulties because of your diminished capacity to function while under stress. Psychotherapy can increase your ability to function without relying on a "crutch" like alcohol, drugs, overeating, anorexia, bulimia, shoplifting, gambling, excessive exercising, self-mutilation, compulsive sexual behavior or some other self-defeating behavior.

Diagnosis of a Psychological Disorder

Consider psychotherapy when a physician has prescribed a Psychotropic medication for you or you have been diagnosed with any of the following common psychological disorders, as found in the Diagnostic and Statistical Manual of Mental Disorders (DSM-IV), published by the American Psychiatric Association:

Depression

You may be depressed if you have five or more of the following: (1) Despondent most of the day for two or more weeks; (2) Loss of pleasure in daily activities; (3) Weight loss or gain of more than 5% when not dieting; (4) Sleeping too little or too much; (5) Fatigue or loss of energy most days; (6) Feeling worthless; (7) Trouble thinking or concentrating; (8) Others observations of you being restless or slowing down; and/or (9) Thinking often about death or suicide.

Anxiety Disorder

You may have an anxiety disorder if you: Have panic attacks, fear crowds or social situations, excessively fear specific objects or situations like snakes or flying, or excessively worry about life events.

Conduct Disorder

You may have conduct disorder if you: Have a persistent pattern of violating the rights of others and violating societal rules and norms such as: (1) Aggression towards people and animals; (2) Destruction of property; (3) Deceitfulness or theft; (4) Serious violation of rules.

Obsessive-Compulsive Disorder

You may be obsessive-compulsive if you have: (1) Consistent preoccupation with ideas, impulses or feelings and/or (2) Repetitive behaviors like hand washing or mental acts like counting.

Impulse Control Disorder

You may have the impulse control disorder such as Kleptomania if you: have recurrent failure to resist stealing objects not needed for personal use or for their monetary value or immediate tension before and pleasure or relief after stealing.

Bi-Polar Disorder

You may have bi-polar disorder if you have had depression and also have: A distinct time of abnormally and elevated irritable or expansive mood that includes at least three of the following: (1) Inflated self-esteem; (2) Pressure to keep talking; (3) Racing thoughts; (4) Easily distracted by unimportant events; (5) Little need for sleep; (6) Increased goal-directed activity or restlessness; (7) Involvement in pleasurable activities to excess (shopping sprees, sex, gambling, shoplifting).

Intermittent Explosive Disorder

You may have intermittent explosive disorder if you have explosive episodes of anger and rage resulting in assault of others or destruction of property.

Personality Disorder

You may have a personality disorder if you: Have a long-term pattern of inner experience and behavior that is inflexible and pervasive in a broad range of personal and social situations. Each of the following is related to a different personality disorder: (1) Having pervasive distrust of others; (2) Detachment from social situations; (3) Discomfort with close personal relationships coupled with odd beliefs and behaviors; (4) Disregard for and violation of the rights of others since age 15; (5) Instability in interpersonal relationships, self-image, and affects; (6) Excessive emotional and attention seeking behavior; (7) Grandiosity, seeking admiration, and lack of empathy; ((8) Social inhibition, feelings of inadequacy and hypersensitivity to negative evaluation; (9) Pervasive need to be taken care of that leads to clinging and submissive behavior; (10) Preoccupation with orderliness, perfectionism, and mental and interpersonal control.

Addictive Personality

You may have an addictive personality if you are compulsive about using alcohol and/or drugs, having affairs, casual sexual encounters, masturbation, gambling, working, watching pornography, shoplifting, using the internet or any other compulsive activity that you cannot stop and causes you problems in relationships and work.

Attachment Disorder

You may have an attachment disorder if you often feel insecurely attached to significant others and feel anxious when a significant other gets emotionally close to you.

Adjustment Disorder

You may have adjustment disorder if a recent life event leads to behavioral and or emotional symptoms such as depression or anxiety.

Even if you have not been diagnosed with a specific disorder, if you are sensitive to the feelings in your body, or aware of some internal struggle or even mildly suspect that talking to a psychotherapist for one or two sessions could be helpful, don't hesitate because of your reluctance to reveal your secrets or because of the money. The benefit could far outweigh the cost.

Some Pros and Cons of Psychotherapy

Pros

1. Psychotherapy vs. short-term counseling or education programs can dig deeper into unresolved issues which may be contributing to your self-defeating behavior. Based on your reading of this book, your awareness and understanding of your issues should be significantly greater than others. Your treatment should therefore be of shorter duration depending upon your level of comprehension.

2. Psychotherapy may be able to identify and treat other issues that could improve the quality of your life.

3. Psychotherapeutic treatment, prior to becoming involved in a possible future incident or arrest, can help to demonstrate you are taking positive steps to alter your behavior. Your therapist could become an advocate in mediation or court proceeding.

4. Psychotherapists could identify and/or prescribe medication(s) which might be appropriate.

Cons

1. The psychotherapist you choose may not have the education, knowledge or experience to effectively treat your specific problem, costing you unnecessary time and money.

2. Try to receive a referral from someone you know and trust with your issue. When you later contact the psychotherapist be proactive and ask if he/she is experienced in handling your type of problem. Ask the psychotherapist his or her understanding of the problem and approach to resolving your issue. If you then feel that the person can help, make an appointment and see how it goes. If you are not satisfied for any reason, discuss it with your therapist and don't hesitate to find a new therapist if that is what you have decided.

3. The long-term nature of psychotherapy vs. short-term treatment with other crisis intervention alternatives could put you more at risk of having a relapse during the treatment period.

4. The cost of psychotherapy, even when partially reimbursed by insurance, is generally far more expensive than qualified short-term treatment programs.

5. The commitment to psychotherapy, which is commonly associated with weekly or semi-weekly scheduling and traveling to office visits, can be difficult for people with two jobs or on a tight weekly schedule.

Medication

Medication may be temporarily helpful in dealing with self-defeating and addictive behaviors.

However, because all medications have some undesirable side effects, it is wise to avoid medication unless truly necessary.

In order to ascertain whether medication may be temporarily helpful for you, consult your primary care physician or a psychiatrist.

CHAPTER 11

Here Is Your
Job For Life

Now that you have almost finished this book, you should be ready to take-on your final job.

With that said, please keep the following things in mind as you navigate your new and improved life:

Recovery from self-defeating behaviors involves simplifying your life.

Primarily it involves recognizing you were born perfect and this will never change, no matter what occurs. Your experiences after birth led you on your path. Recovery involves rebuilding trust in yourself so that you make all decisions for you. It involves seeing and replacing previously held *false beliefs* with the *real truth*, and using your own internal guidance system by allowing your inner wisdom to be in harmony with the outer experiences in your world.

Said another way, always remember that nothing is wrong with you as a human being, only trust yourself, replace any *false beliefs* you acquired in life with the *real truth* and allow your own built-in "Guidance System" to keep you on course.

Remember How Self-Defeating Behaviors Develop

Self-defeating behaviors develop as the result of holding onto false beliefs because one doesn't trust or value oneself enough to see and explore better alternatives.

Self-defeating behaviors develop because shameful secrets are given too much importance by the secret's holder and thereby inhibit these individuals from moving forward.

Self-defeating behaviors are permitted to take hold in people who falsely believe they are somehow broken, damaged or defeated, and therefore unable to rise to what otherwise would be their true self.

Self-defeating behaviors develop when one feels confused and unable to identify and satisfy their fundamental human needs and seeks alternatives in a self-defeating way.

Self-defeating behaviors develop when people are afraid to act honestly because they anticipate an unfavorable reaction or believe they cannot control the outcome of events. All they really need to do is be respectful, don't attempt to control, stay in balance and harmony with all things recognizing there are always alternatives.

Self-defeating behaviors frequently result in people who are depressed.

A HIDDEN ADDICTION exists when you are not aware that you have become so dependent on something or someone that you must always act to satisfy your dependence.

Here Is Your Job For Life

Daily Checklist

EVERYDAY, remember all the following thoughts to ensure you are living the positive life you want. These thoughts represent a short reminder of what you have read in this book. As you accept and practice these thoughts day in and day out, they will become automatic and require little, if any, further attention.

1. Face your secrets (within yourself) and recognize there is a specific reason (not an excuse) why things happened the way they did in your life. Your acceptance will allow you to open your eyes and mind to see the *real truth* within. Based on the positive images you will eventually see, promise yourself that you will not allow your secret(s) to haunt or shame you for the rest of your life.

2. Remember you are a *good person* who has experienced difficult times, but that you are working to make your

life better. Be proud of each accomplishment rather than focusing on past mistakes.

3. Remember that your past behavior was just a *"symptom" or "signal"* to you that you were having difficulty with your ability to cope with the pressures you faced. Your self-defeating behaviors did not reflect who you are as a person.

4. Remember that you were born as a *perfect* human being and that can never change. Accept you are not flawed in any way and never be ashamed of who you are. Apologize when you are wrong and graciously accept compliments when they are deserved.

5. Remember that the mistakes you made and will make through trial and error are a natural part of learning for all of us. Be grateful you are now a wiser person because of your experiences and the help you received.

6. Remember that your past experiences are in the past (gone forever) and can never be in your present or future *unless you allow them in.*

7. Recognize that your *four basic needs* must *always remain unthreatened.* Any stress you feel will most likely be perceived as a threat to one or more of your needs for either *safety, love relationships, your independence and freedom, or your self-worth.* This recognition will lead you to the solution.

8. Accept that life throws us curveballs and that *your response* (not the curves thrown) is what makes

the difference in the outcome and quality of your life.

9. *Trust yourself* and not others to know what is best for you.

10. Remember that *fear* and *control* are an illusion. Discard fear based on the false belief that things are trying to hurt you. Respect the special characteristics and natural differences within all things so they don't clash in some way. Discard the idea that you can control living things. Rather, endeavor to be in harmony with them. Continue to seek perfection in life by keeping your life balanced. In life, perfection is the achievement of balance.

11. Remember the *hurt, blame & anger* equation. Release your blame of others who you perceive hurt you and replace it with the *"real truth"* in each situation. The truth may be that you need to make amends in some way for your past actions or your recognition that the other person has an individual problem. This will release the anger which can lead to depression.

The *real truth* is often just the application of common sense.

12. Use both parts of your God-given internal guidance system to get the answers you are looking for by *listening to your body*. Your body knows the real truth; it never lies to you and communicates

the truth to you in the form of thoughts and feelings.

13. Never proceed with anything unless you're rational and emotional parts of your guidance system are both aligned and in agreement. This is usually accomplished in a matter of seconds.

14. Identify and replace "*false beliefs*" about yourself or others with the "*real truth.*" We all know the real truth when we are willing to see it.

15. Remember that when you finally accept the *real truth* it will immediately replace the *false belief* you once held. This will allow you to no longer be guided by an illusion.

16. Seek *ongoing support* whenever you feel the need in order to keep you focused. Keep your eye on the ball to prevent you from dropping it.

17. Finally, it is nice to remember that we are all wiser and more capable than we realize.

(Don't lose sight of the fact that all this is connected to self-defeating behaviors.)

You Might Like To Know:

What Do I Try To Do When I Have The Kind Of Problems We All Experience?

While it is difficult to know precisely what I would do in a given situation, I have a pretty good idea I would like to share with you.

If I have a problem with my health, my wife's disappointment in me, my son's stern handling of my grandchild (in my opinion), my loss of confidence in myself because of rejection of my proposals to others, or any other problem, I would take the following steps:

First, I would try to calm down from any initial impulse or feeling of sadness, anger, rage or unworthiness.

Second, I would say to myself, 'What is really going on here?' or 'How important is this?' This will help to balance my emotions with my intelligence. For example, I would say to myself, "Is my health problem temporary or permanent? Is my health prognosis favorable or unknown and do I want to jump the gun and worry before there is a need to worry? Is my wife correct and do I need to apologize to her or is she overacting to her own fears or did I just push one of her buttons? What does my son need to know in order to properly handle the problem with my grandchild and what is the best way to approach this delicate subject they could perceive as criticism, even though they should realize that my motives come from my deep caring about them and my grandchild?

Third, if I am in emotional distress, I would immediately identify which one of my four basic needs are being threatened and consider whether the threat is real and the actions I should take to feel less threatened.

Fourth, I would remind myself the solution to almost any problem rests within me and usually has a number of possible approaches, while always remembering to be sincere, truthful, caring or loving (vs. annoyed or critical), remain self-confident, trust my feelings, be willing to accept life's proven realties, don't try to fool myself into believing what I want to be true, help loved ones to understand the situation and don't wait too long or be ashamed to ask for support if I think I might need it.

Be Well and Best Wishes,
Peter Berlin
Peter@PeterBerlinAddictionCoach.com

About the Author

Peter Berlin has appeared on national TV, radio, in magazines and news media for over 30 years as a person who initially apprehended and interviewed shoplifters in retail stores and later founded the first national non-profit organization to help rehabilitate offenders.

After receiving a BS degree in Psychology from Long Island University, Mr. Berlin later began working in retail stores interviewing shoplifters and dishonest employees and began to discover how many otherwise decent people engage in self-defeating behaviors without ever understanding why ... or how to resolve their addictive patterns. He later discovered that the same stress, overreaction and inability to cope that lead people to shoplift is also replicated in other self-defeating behaviors.

Mr. Berlin later began working with prosecutors, judges and probation personnel in juvenile and criminal courts to enroll shoplifters into education programs which he developed with a staff of psychologists. His national education programs have been accepted in thousands of courts in 46 states.

Mr. Berlin also joined the prestigious Price Waterhouse firm and became the head of international consulting on retail theft to more than 100 retail firms worldwide. He published international monthly newsletters for 24 years.

Mr. Berlin is a speaker, writer and addiction coach on the resolution of self-defeating behaviors.

APPENDIX I

Wallet Card

Because there are a number of things to remember in order to avoid becoming involved with or eliminating self-defeating behaviors, I have prepared a card for you to carry in your wallet.

Cut-out the card on the dotted lines, fold the four sections into one and place it into your wallet.

Read your card every morning before you start your day.

Keep the Wallet Card with you until you know that your self-defeating behaviors are gone.

"The HIDDEN ADDICTION Behind Self-Defeating Behaviors"

A HIDDEN ADDICTION exists when you are not aware that you have become so dependent on something or someone that you must always act to satisfy your dependence.

Remember How Self-Defeating Behaviors Develop?

- Failing to recognize and accept that you were born a "perfect" human being and you can never change what God and Mother Nature created.
- Failing to recognize and accept your own goodness, value and self-worth.
- Holding onto shameful secrets about self.
- Holding onto "false beliefs" about self and not replacing them with the "truth".
- Believing you are damaged, broken, defeated, incapable.
- Allowing others to decide what is best for you instead of only trusting yourself.
- Not connecting problems to your 4 fundamental needs.
- Not listening to your built-in Guidance System.
- Holding onto unrealistic blame and anger resulting in depression.
- Acting fearful, controlling and unbalanced rather than being in harmony and respectful toward your world.

How Does One Eliminate Self-Defeating Behaviors?

- Recognize that you are a worthy human being.
- Recognize and accept the real goodness within you.
- Release and resolve shameful secrets about self.
- Replace "false beliefs" about self with the "real truth".
- Know that you are not damaged, broken, defeated or incapable.
- Only trust yourself to make all decisions for you.
- Connect all problems to your 4 fundamental needs.
- Listen to your built-in Guidance System.
- Eliminate unrealistic anger (depression) by eliminating blame.
- Be in harmony (show respect) for all things and don't allow yourself to fear, control or unbalance your world.

Wallet Card
BACK

"The HIDDEN ADDICTION Behind Self-Defeating Behaviors"

Daily Checklist:

EVERYDAY, remember all the following thoughts to ensure you are living the positive life you want. As you accept and practice these thoughts day in and day out, they will become automatic and require little, if any, further attention.

- Face your secrets (within yourself) and recognize there is a specific reason (not an excuse) why things happened the way they did in your life. See the truth. Your acceptance will no longer allow your secret(s) to haunt or shame you for the rest of your life.

- Remember you are a good person who has experienced difficult times, but that you are working to make your life better. Be proud of each accomplishment rather than focusing on past mistakes.

- Remember that your past behavior was just a "symptom" or "signal" to you that you were having difficulty with your ability to cope with the pressures you faced. Your self-defeating behaviors do not reflect who you really are as a person.

- Remember that you were born as a perfect human being and that will never change. Accept you are not flawed in any way and never be ashamed of who you are. Apologize when you are wrong and graciously accept compliments when they are deserved.

- Remember that the mistakes you made and will make through trial and error are a natural part of learning for all of us. Be grateful you are now a wiser person because of your experiences and the help you received.

- Remember that your past experiences are in the past (gone forever) and can never be in your present or future unless you allow them in.

- Accept that life throws us curveballs and that your response (not the curves thrown) is what makes the difference in the outcome and quality of your life.

- Trust yourself and not others to know what is best for you.

- Remember that fear and control are illusions. Discard fear based on the false belief that things are trying to hurt you. Respect the special characteristics and natural differences within all things so they don't clash in some way and endeavor to be in harmony with them. Continue to seek perfection in life by keeping your life balanced. In life, perfection is perfect balance.

- Remember the hurt, blame & anger equation. Release your blame of others who you perceive hurt you and replace it with the "real truth" in each situation. This will release the anger which can lead to depression. The real truth is often just the application of common sense.

- Use both parts of your God-given internal guidance system to get the answers you are looking for by listening to your body. Your body knows the real truth, it never lies to you and communicates the truth to you in the form of thoughts and feelings.

- Never proceed with anything unless you're rational and emotional parts of your guidance system are both aligned and in agreement. This is usually accomplished in a matter of seconds.

- Identify and replace "false beliefs" about yourself or others with the "real truth." We all know the real truth when we are willing to see it.

- Remember that when you finally accept the real truth it will immediately replace the false belief you once held. This will allow you to no longer be guided by an illusion.

- Seek ongoing support whenever you feel the need in order to keep you focused.

- Finally, it is nice to remember that we are all wiser and more capable than we realize.

(Don't lose sight of the fact that all this is connected to self-defeating behaviors.)

Contact us anytime:
www.PeterBerlinAuthor-AddictionCoach.com
or email **Peter@PeterBerlinAddictionCoach.com**

APPENDIX II

Complimentary Report: "Why Did You Shoplift?"

available at
www.PeterBerlinShopliftingCoach.com

If you wish to receive more information or a complimentary report containing answers about the problem of shoplifting, go to the website listed above.

APPENDIX III

Direct Quotes From Individuals Receiving Telephone Coaching

The following are direct quotes taken from letters written about or to Mr. Berlin after conducting one or more telephone coaching sessions with people who have a problem with shoplifting. The coaching sessions provided participants with a way to apply the material in this book to their unique personal life. They are listed here to give the reader a sense of value that people feel they receive from the material discussed in his book.

"Mr. Berlin … thank you for your help. It was a great feeling after 32 years of living with this problem in secret to be able to open up to someone who understands and feels what I am going through. ... Yes, I HAVE A PROBLEM!!! ... But thanks to you and your organization at least now I have the tools and the knowledge to deal with it ... which is something I never had before.

—J.P., Murieta, CA

"Prior to my coaching sessions with you I was feeling so much shame, emptiness, grief and worthlessness. I have made it (so far) without shoplifting. I feel very proud of myself and feel very liberated every time I walk out of a store. ... I feel stronger than I have in years. ... Now I have the tools to help myself avoid shoplifting and I have a solid plan to walk safely through my life from this point on. ... Thank you very much for your support and understanding.

—N.A.M., Tulalip, WA

"Thank you so much for spending time on the phone with me and helping me to see things more clearly through the eyes of TRUTH and not the lies I have become accustomed to. ... Thank God for you and your work. I wish I knew about you earlier and that there is hope with support."

—P.D.,Clifton Spring, NY

"I was feeling depressed after a recent argument with my husband ... I had gained weight from having my daughter ... he didn't find me sexy ... I felt unwanted and ugly. After getting the serious help I needed from Mr. Berlin and my therapist ... I stopped shoplifting by utilizing the tools they have given me. In the past, I had never had any help with my problem since it was all too embarrassing to talk about."

—*J.S., Santa Rosa, CA*

"The sessions with Mr. Berlin were amazing … after having three sessions with him my thought pattern has changed. I have been given specific tools to deal with any temptation and he has helped me understand why I started in the first place. His prognosis for me is good and he has written a letter on my behalf expressing this."

—*S.G., Dallas, TX*

"Wow, thank you for your kind words and for all your support. Your letter to the court was amazing."

—*Q.C., Winnepeg, Canada*

"Mr. Berlin … Thanks and I am still clean and will remain clean."

—*R.E.B., Ventura, CA*

"Mr. Berlin … Thank you for your help and advice about my problem. I have been trying to find an explanation … I feel that after I talk to you … this embarrassing problem it won't happen to me again."

—*J.R., Phoenix, AZ*

"Thank you for your insight and time. It was great to have the pieces put together, I had never thought about these things before like this."

—*B.Y., Madison, WI*

"Peter ... Well, I must say that you were able to diagnose what was going on with me and why I did what I did. ... I thought it was interesting right off the bat – just the way I talked in the beginning of the conversation you could see I lacked in self-confidence. ... Obviously, I was self-medicating myself when I shoplifted. ... I should have taken the course and spoken with you the first time I was caught shoplifting."

—*S.P., Lakeview, OH*

"I definitely feel that the telephone session helped me. ... Thank you, Mr. Berlin, for really caring about my situation and genuinely wanting to help me out. ... I guarantee that I will never do this again. ... I don't think it will be easy but knowing what I know now, I will be able to make the right choices."

—*T.Y., Rock Spring, WY*

"Mr. Berlin ... I just cannot believe that it is 1:05 a.m. and you are up doing something so selfless in efforts to assist me in my recovery. I cannot believe how truly caring you are. ... Please understand, Mr. Berlin, I am not accustomed to someone really being there for me. This is a 'first time' and I will never forget ... I promise not to let myself or you down."

—*S.P., Philadelphia, PA*

"The NASP course as well as the over the phone coaching session has really opened my eyes to changes that I need to make for myself – changes that I can and will make in order to be the real person that I am, not the person I was during this dark time of my life. Thank you from the bottom of my heart for helping me ... Shoplifting is not part of who I am.

—*T.G., Bronx, NY*

"Going through a divorce, enormous amount of debt and my bitter ex bashing me orally to my three children, I felt as though I needed to stay in positive good graces with my children ... I shoplifted items for them, items I felt I could not afford. ... I now have a clearer realization of what these effects and stress's have created in my mind ... I now can better fight the temptations to shoplift."

—*D.M., Cypress, CA*

"Thank you for our phone coaching session today. You helped me immensely! I appreciate your helpful suggestions regarding a new start and replacing behaviors. I have already had five successful days without any shoplifting and look forward to never, ever doing it again."

—*T.L., Jasper, GA*

"Mr. Berlin ...thank you for the extra time you took in speaking with my mother. She thought you were fantastic! ... We went to lunch after the coaching and we talked about her four pages of notes she took. The next day she cooked dinner for Father's Day and seemed more alive. I would love to arrange for her to speak to you once a week."

—*D.F., Staten Island, NY*

"I am so grateful that you took the time to speak with me and I feel that I really benefitted from your guidance. … Your words made me feel better about myself … since my apprehension. I felt that our conversation gave me the confidence to take a proactive stand on my crime. … Thank you for empowering me."

—*V.N., Brooklyn, NY*

"Dear Peter … It was so uplifting talking to you last night. … I was at an all-time 'low' when I got arrested. … I can and will control this addiction.

—*L.W., Wonderlake, IL*

"I am sure that with all the insights I have gained, it will be easier to STOP. I am glad you are only a phone call away if I need your help and that's a good thing."

—*B.Mc, Lincoln Park, MI*

"I became more in control seeking the help I need".

—*K.J., Houston, TX*

"Mr. Berlin … I have learned a life-long lesson from our phone conversation. … I will never shoplift again. … I have replaced my 'emotional' pain with integrity and intelligence.

… And that is how I have rehabilitated myself. … Thank you from the bottom of my heart."

—*C.N., Huntington Beach, CA*

"I had never stolen or considered shoplifting in my entire life. However, after a week of pressure, I finally caved in. After taking the NASP course and speaking with you (Peter Berlin), I have recognized and learned a few things. … In retrospect it is a very good thing that I was caught. … I, with complete sincerity, know this will never happen again. … Thank you so much for your time and willingness to help me."

—*C.S., Olathe, KS*

"Thank you again for our session this week. It has helped me to understand how my behavior is an act of expression of my need for anxiety release due to traumatic experiences in my past… Once I … change my perspective of these traumatic events, I believe that my shoplifting addiction will no longer be a compulsion."

—*C.C., Portsmouth, NH*

"After talking to you I got the help I needed. I can see clear and I'm in control of my feelings and behavior. I am so glad I made that phone call … I have a new beginning now, full of hope and feeling better than yesterday about myself … Thanks Peter Berlin for making me see myself a lot better than I did in the past."

—*C.S., Van Nuys, CA*

"Mr. Berlin ... I found our session to be very helpful. I am used to being independent, but speaking to someone about my feelings and thoughts help to clarify mistakes I am making in the way I approach issues in life, and teach me ways to handle stress and depression. Thank you."

—*J.S., Greenwich, CT*

"Thank you so much Mr. Berlin for your help. I know now that my reasons for shoplifting related to unresolved emotional and personal issues. I am happy to know that you are available to help me at any time."

—*M.D., Pittsburgh, PA*

"It was a pleasure going through this eye opening experience with you today. ... After taking the Assessment and speaking to you, I have identified why I was shoplifting. Thank you for your time and help."

—*T.E.J., Alexandra, VA*

"I will never do it again. I know now how to be happy with what I have and how to cope with stress in my life."

—*J.P., Folsom, CA*

CPSIA information can be obtained
at www.ICGtesting.com
Printed in the USA
JSHW030601101220
10138JS00002B/100